Six Qualities
of
WOMEN
of
Character

As for the saints who are in the land,
they are the glorious ones in whom is all my delight.

Psalm 16:3

Six Qualities
of
WOMEN
of
Character

Life-Changing Examples
of Godly Women

DEBRA EVANS

ZondervanPublishingHouse
Grand Rapids, Michigan

A Division of HarperCollins*Publishers*

Requests for information should be addressed to:

 ZondervanPublishingHouse
Grand Rapids, Michigan 49530

Library of Congress Cataloging-in-Publication Data

Evans, Debra.
    Women of character: life-changing examples of godly women / Debra Evans.
        p. cm.
    Includes bibliographical references (p.).
    ISBN: 0–310–20153–5 (hardcover)
    1. Christian women—Religious life.   2. Women in the Bible.   3. Christian
women—Biography.   I. Title.
BV4527.E89   1996
248.8'43-dc20   95–41865
                                                  CIP

This edition printed on acid-free paper and meets the American National Standards
Institute Z39.48 standard.

Published in association with Wolgemuth & Hyatt, Inc.

Edited by Mary McCormick
Interior design by Sherri L. Hoffman

Printed in the United States of America

---

95 96 97 98 99 00 01 02 /❖ DH/ 10 9 8 7 6 5 4 3 2 1

For Barbara Pett

Contents

Acknowledgments

I am grateful to have a conscientious contingent of friends who always seem to know exactly when I will most value their letters, phone calls, gifts, notecards, stop-by visits, and luncheon invitations. Some of their stories are in this book. A handful of these people and I have known each other for twenty-five years, or longer; others, I have become acquainted with since relocating to Texas in the summer of 1993. At various times, we have supported one another during periods of personal struggle and painful spiritual growth. I prize their prayers and perceptions.

A warm and heartfelt thanks goes to Sandra Vander Zicht for her expert professional guidance, editorial oversight, and publishing ingenuity, and to my editor (and mother of six!), Mary McCormick, for her skilled and intuitive service as the book's "midwife" during the final stages of labor. To art director Jody Langley, I extend my enthusiastic gratitude for designing *Women of Character*'s elegant cover and sending it by overnight mail only three days before her wedding. And, though I do not know most of their names, I want to convey my genuine regard for the Zondervan staffpersons — the secretaries, computer specialists, proofreaders, typesetters, publishing committee members, marketing consultants, shipping-room workers, and many others — who carried out essential production, promotion, or distribution tasks.

I have also been consistently aided by my literary support team, Wolgemuth & Hyatt, Inc., to whom I express my appreciation for their creative direction and encouragement over the past six years: Mike Hyatt, for introducing me to Pelagia's story, affirming my vocation, and setting an example for others to follow; Cheryl Richards, for making timely phone follow-ups and finding answers to my questions; Robert Wolgemuth, for contributing his capable direction; and Martin Culpepper, for persistently coordinating last year's efforts and filling in the blanks.

Most important, I want to thank my family, to whom I am indebted for their love and caring support:

— my sister Kerry, for coming to Austin during Advent and, a few months later, offering the gift of a plane ticket after the manuscript was completed;

— my sister Nancy, for sending thoughtful cards, visiting in the midst of her busy schedule, and making regular "just checking in" phone calls;

— my parents, John and Nancy, for urging me to bring the family along for an extended summer stay at their lakeside home in northern Michigan, and for their faithful prayers each morning;

— my daughters, Joanna and Katy, for expressing their fiery spiritual enthusiasm, honest insight, and stubborn loving-kindness with a mom who often asks them to wait until later;

— my sons, David and Jon, and (son-in-law) Matthew, for telling me their hopes and dreams, making me smile, learning to take responsibility where it counts — and being willing to wait on themselves;

— my granddaughter, Abigail, for sharing her endlessly entertaining funny faces, incomparable hugs, and inspiring determination;

— and, as always, my husband, Dave, for providing his steady generosity, insomnia-curing guitar serenades, sage wisdom, creative home cuisine (particularly, salmon pancakes with fresh chives and Mexi-Pizza Pinwheels), daily cactus tours, detailed lessons on shaping human service delivery models, and a surprising pledge to join me on the journey some twenty-six years ago, on the second Saturday of our spring break.

Introduction

> The ashes of martyrs drive away demons.[1]
> — St. John Chrysostom (ca. 345–407)

This book is meant to encourage spiritual endurance by telling the stories of twelve biblical and classical women whom the Lord loved. But it is also about six divinely supplied "graces" — brokenness, belief, surrender, obedience, devotion, and service — that help us to rely on Christ's strength instead of our own.

The condition of our hearts creates a continual need for ongoing confession and forgiveness, for turning away from sin and receiving God's mercy. Challenging life circumstances can quickly sidetrack spiritual growth. But we are not alone: The Scriptures show us, by example, how women of faith faced shame and were freed from bondage, lost a husband and moved on, surrendered their comfort and gained God's kingdom. In the Bible, we see women with a past transformed into women of character.

The Bible reminds us that we are surrounded by "a great cloud of witnesses" (Hebrews 12:1) from whom we are to gain encouragement as we run toward the finish line of our faith. As we read their stories, recognize their struggles, and imagine their victories, we find courage. In his book *The Fight*, Christian psychiatrist Dr. John White invites us to picture it this way: "Moses is at your elbow as you approach the starting point. So are Joshua and Rahab the harlot. So, too, are thousands of unknowns who went through hell on earth and proved God true. They are straining to speak to you, to tell you something; and about someone . . ."[2]

The purpose of this book is to link this rich legacy from the past to our lives today. The experiences of Abigail, Mary of Bethany, and others still teach us about how God's power, love,

11

and mercy work for good in our lives. Asking ourselves, "Which biblical (or classical Christian) woman do I identify most with right now?" can point us in a new direction when the road ahead seems unpromising or dim. Understanding how God aids and enables us to move ahead by providing us with special graces, a term used by earlier saints to signify the Holy Spirit's "helps" (not to be confused with the singular word *grace*, which means God's unmerited favor), reminds us to open our hands to receive what only our heavenly Father can give us, to take time to rest in His presence, and to find joy in being alone with Jesus.

Two years ago, on a visit to the New College chapel at Oxford University, I was stunned to discover a collection of marble sculptures, arranged in successive rows of orderly tiers, stacked from the floor to the ceiling on the front wall of the small church. There they were, prophets, martyrs, apostles, angels, Christ on the cross, and above all, the Lamb of God, with faces depicting a peculiar determination to look beyond present realities toward heaven. History tells us that several of these saints were burned at the stake because of their beliefs; some were crucified; others, beheaded.

Seeing this noble assembly of heroes represented before me was almost overwhelming. Surprised by the scene, I silently considered how this long-ago company had lived and died and now lives again in God's presence, an unexpected reminder of an extraordinary hope in the midst of a Saturday sight-seeing tour. The chorus of heaven's company awakened in me a longing to know more about my Christian family ancestors.

Although I was already well-acquainted with biblical heroes such as Rahab, Ruth, and Mary of Magdala, I knew little about later Christian champions — women like Vibia Perpetua, a young mother, patriarch's daughter, and early Roman martyr; Pandita Ramabai, one of India's greatest social and spiritual reformers; and Amanda Smith, an American born into slavery who grew up to become an internationally acclaimed evangelist. Through the testimony of their lives, I have been amazed and inspired by the possibilities true belief affords. From these women I have acquired a fresh perspective on Christian beauty, "the inner personality —

the unfading loveliness of a calm and gentle spirit, a thing very precious in the eyes of God" (1 Peter 3:4–5 PHILLIPS). As I look into the lives of women who went before me, I see the image and character of God reflected in their brave, trusting hearts — women who were willing to grow up into their full stature as the saints we are *all* becoming. It is as if, by their radiant witness, they are vigorously inviting each of us to let go of our fear and doubt as we move into a mysterious future where we do not necessarily know the answers.

If it has not been your practice to read about saints' lives, I invite you to view these holy women as historical witnesses to the glory of God, whose memorable victories bring us strong support. Rather than react to past abuses of their testimonies, we may choose instead to freely embrace their heroic, sisterly examples of faith in a fresh and different way today.

In *Women of Character*, you will find a collection of themes to consider as you examine and exercise your faith, and, in doing so, build your spiritual endurance. Each chapter opens with a few "case histories" — firsthand accounts of contemporary women's still-to-be-resolved struggles — and how acceptance, or refusal, of a particular grace has affected their relationship with God.[3] These stories introduce the Christian quality I present and bring to life our timely need for strenuous reliance on the Holy Spirit's helps. Then the focus shifts. Two saintly women's testimonies, one taken directly from the Scriptures and one borrowed from various historical accounts, apply the grace under discussion. Quotations, Bible verses, related poems, hymn lyrics, prayers, and reflection points further emphasize the chapter's central theme.

This book is a small volume designed to be savored and digested slowly, intended for highlighting favorite passages and journaling in the margins. It is my hope that you will be helped and encouraged as you read these pages.

Chapter One

Brokenness

∴ 🍇 ∼

Is there anything more joyful here on earth
than the grace of contrition and repentance? Can we
reach for anything greater than this grace?[1]
— M. Basilea Schlink, *Repentance — the Joy-filled Life*

*J*esus said, "Blessed are the poor in spirit, for theirs is the
kingdom of heaven" (Matt. 5:3). Another translation proclaims, "Happy are those who know their need for God, for the
kingdom of heaven is theirs!" (Matt. 5:3 PHILLIPS) In his psalm of
penitence, King David expressed the value of spiritual poverty
this way: "A broken and contrite heart, O God, you will not
despise" (Ps. 51:17).

Look up the word *contrition* — the classical term for brokenness — in your dictionary. It is taken from a Latin word meaning
"to wear down or grind to pieces." Not exactly an appealing discussion topic. Most of us aim for the mountaintop-type experiences, the spiritual high places. Perhaps it is because we assume
that is where we are closer to the Creator, but the Bible teaches
something different: It is when we have been broken up into tiny
bits that we are close to our Father's heart. Brokenness opens the
door for deeper fellowship with God.

Through the ages, many Christians have been convinced of
the spiritual necessity for contrition. "The most certain indication
of our improvement is to be convinced of our misery," advised
Jean-Pierre de Caussade, an eighteenth-century French convent
counselor, in one of his *Spiritual Letters.* "In this way we shall be
richer as we imagine we are poorer, and we shall be more humble

15

within, more mistrustful of ourselves and more disposed to con-
fide in God alone."[2]

With nothing left to hide, our eyes open wider. We cannot fool
ourselves any longer: We need Jesus to enter our broken places
and mend our fractured hearts.

For my friend Erin, the grace of brokenness arrived unexpectedly at the end of a Sunday morning church service. I heard
her go forward right after the pastor issued the invitation: "If there
is anyone here who would like to receive special prayer today,
please join me up front," he said. "I'd like to pray for you today."

Perhaps I should not have opened my eyes then, but I knew
what Erin had been going through, and because I was sitting directly
behind her, it had become impossible for me to ignore her pain.

As she kneeled near the altar, I saw the tears fill Erin's eyes;
soon, the trickle turned into a torrent. Silently praying for God to
strengthen my friend's heart, I recalled her recent confession: She
had been secretly involved in an affair with a married man at our
church, a mutual friend's husband, for over a year. Two spouses'
hearts had been broken. Both families' foundations were trembling. Their broken spirits desperately needed a remedy.

I strongly suspected that the Devil's destructive strategies
would not be successful at the end, especially if those of us standing by, ready to lend a hand, had any say in the matter. My friend's
story was not over. God's good would work together with this
wrong for the sake of His Son's loved ones.

Looking at Erin once more, I saw healing in progress, and
kept praying.

For another friend, Kathryn, the grace of brokenness arrived
in an entirely different guise. A Christian for over two decades,
Kathryn had exhausted her natural supply of spiritual strength.
"I have nothing left to give," she bluntly announced one afternoon.
"After all these years, I really don't feel any further ahead in my
ability to love others the way that Jesus did. In fact, I've come to
the conclusion that there's *nothing* here that's good," Kathryn said
emphatically, placing her hand over her heart and staring straight
into my eyes. "Apart from God, I know — and, I mean, I *truly*
know — I'm still completely incapable of that kind of love."

This was not a game. Kathryn was perfectly serious. Here was someone who, for quite a long time now, I had identified as a faithful follower of Jesus, a woman to whom being a Christian is a way of life.

What was she saying to me?

Puzzled by my friend's stark, out-of-the-blue admission, I decided to keep listening. I could tell by Kathryn's reflective expression that she had ventured far into unexplored spiritual territory. Where was she heading? I encouraged her to keep talking.

"I'm not even sure if I can describe it, exactly," Kathryn admitted. "I feel so worn out. What I've become convinced of is that what I've been doing for a long time now is this: trying to be a good Christian by drawing upon my own resources and talents instead of waiting upon God, empty-handed, for as long as it takes, and saying to Him, 'Who am I kidding? I give up! I cannot do it! I don't *care* about people the way You do, Lord — and I get angry and feel frustrated and end up exhausted trying to prove I can.'

"Sure, I'm nice — it's my self-made means of staying in control," Kathryn told me. "But it isn't love."

Thank heaven for honest friends.

"My error hasn't been obvious, but it's been deeply destructive, and I feel inwardly broken," my companion continued to explain. "Consequently, I've decided to pull back for a while — no new activities, lots of solitude, low profile at church, extended periods of prayer."

Then she quietly said, "I guess I've finally realized that I've been relying too heavily on my own resources and not enough on the Lord's strong love — as if good works and being nice to people equals eternal treasure."

"But don't these things matter too?" I wondered, out loud.

"Of course. They're vitally important. But you can serve God with very little real reliance on Christ, as I often have, without regularly waiting upon Him in private to refill your cup. Committees and a full schedule aren't what I'm thirsty for. I've been depending on my natural talents and abilities, instead of God, for long enough. It's time for a change."

Nothing left to give. Empty-handed. Broken. Thirsty. Had I heard the words correctly? For Kathryn, a modern evangelical Protestant, there was no familiar frame of reference to fit her current experience into. Yet, according to traditional Christian teaching, what she was describing was not a full-blown spiritual crisis but contrition — a sudden awakening to the dried-up, empty desert in her heart.

If, like Erin, we are faced with sin's painful consequences, or discover the alarming fact of our spiritual poverty, as Kathryn did — whether we find contrition after years of wandering in the wilderness or after a single cataclysmic event that shatters every notion of our inner goodness — the grace of brokenness moves us toward true humility.

God's unfailing love is most powerfully revealed to us as we meet Him in the midst of our broken, bulldozed, bottomed-out places. In the following story about Mary of Magdala, we see why.

Mary of Magdala's Story

We know so little about her. But three clues point toward what happened later.

When we first meet Mary of Magdala, we discover that she is a devoted follower and friend of Jesus, traveling about "from one village to another" with the Lord and His disciples. This is extraordinary, isn't it? Hebrew men and women were not supposed to worship in close proximity, and rabbis certainly did not select female students for co-ed tutelage. Women heard religious teaching from afar, in a synagogue, behind a curtain, maybe. But Jewish wives and mothers temporarily leaving their homes to participate as respected team players on a mobile ministry crew? Never. At least, not until the amazing events recorded by the apostles in New Testament times took place.

Following this brief, scene-setting introduction, we are next told that someone in Jesus' group, "Mary, known as the 'woman from Magdala'" (Luke 8:2 PHILLIPS), was once possessed by seven demons.

Mary's suffering prior to her deliverance must have been enormous. Incomprehensible, really. Though we are not informed about the exact nature of her spiritual affliction, we know that Jesus had set her free. And Mary of Magdala's allegiance to Christ consistently demonstrated her lasting gratitude.

Yet, of the many adjectives used to describe her, the word *loyal* rarely springs to most people's minds first. Nothing in the Bible connects Mary with the penitent prostitute portrayed elsewhere in the Gospels, and the Scriptures never state that her spiritual bondage was specifically sexual. For all we know, her demonic possession may have been the origin of emotional or physical illness, wrecking Mary's life as it played havoc with her mind and body.

Regardless of what her afflictions were, we actually know very little about Mary's past. What is important is that Jesus gave her a clean start. To Mary, Jesus — the Man she followed, saw crucified, and waited for next to the tomb — was more than a regular working rabbi. He was her healer and beloved teacher (John 20:16).

In addition to traveling with Jesus and receiving instruction from Him, there is one more thing worth noting about His special student: Mary appears to have been a woman of independent means, possibly as a result of a family inheritance or widowhood. Her money allowed her to accompany Jesus and provide support to His ministry. The Scriptures show that Mary did not join the group simply to take but to give generously, listing her first among many women who supported Jesus and the twelve disciples "out of their own means" (Luke 8:3).

Near the Cross

This is how we know what love is: Jesus Christ
laid down his life for us. 1 John 3:16

*O*f all Christ's family and followers, only five stood near Jesus at the cross on Golgotha: John, His beloved disciple; His mother, Mary, and her sister, Mary, Clopas's wife; a woman named Salome; and Mary of Magdala. Other believers, many of them women, watched from somewhere close by. But the Bible only specifically mentions these five.

Some of Jesus' camp, no doubt, had scattered across Jerusalem or were hiding in the surrounding hills, taking refuge from the sights and sounds of creation's groans as the earth heaved, the wind roared, and the sky, temporarily struck sunless, turned upside down. Saints, after all, are only human.

But Mary of Magdala refused to turn and run. She chose not to leave Jesus alone with His accusers and executioners. Neither the gruesome scene of Christ's crucifixion, saturated with darkness and desolation as it was, nor the threat of personal persecution and punishment were enough to sever Mary's fidelity to the Lord.

Surely, her faith met its ultimate test that day. How could anyone who loved Jesus have remained unshaken by the sickening spectacle?

Watching a loved one die is an agonizing experience. Added to the anguish of seeing her dearest friend killed before her eyes, Mary knew that an innocent Man was being slaughtered. Every year, on Good Friday, we look back in repentance and remember. But she was *there*.

The Bible says, "For he has forgiven us all our sins; he has canceled the bond which pledged us to the decrees of the law. It stood against us, but he has set it aside, nailing it to the cross" (Col. 2:14 NEB). As Mary watched Jesus suffer, did she realize the Lord's death was the final atonement for her sin too?

We frequently recall our Savior's sacrifice on behalf of sinners. Mary of Magdala saw the nails pierce His flesh. There was nothing she could do to save Him.

He was there to save her.

At the Tomb

The world and its desires pass away, but the man who does the will of God lives forever. 1 John 2:17

After Jesus died, Mary accompanied Nicodemus and Joseph of Arimathea, a secret disciple, as they carried the Lord's body to the tomb. Nicodemus brought a mixture of myrrh and aloes, weighing over seventy-five pounds, to place in the linen burial wrappings — a symbolic gesture of his love and devotion for the Lord. The two men hurriedly performed the proper ritual. It was near sunset, the beginning of the Sabbath, when their work would be over.

Grief-stricken and in shock, Mary was still there, sitting across from the tomb with Jesus' aunt, when the men finished their heartrending task. She did not leave until after Jesus' remains had been laid to rest and were securely sealed by a sizable boulder that Joseph rolled across the sepulcher's entrance.

Jesus was dead. And by all appearances, Mary of Magdala did not expect the Savior to rise from His stony grave.

How brokenhearted Mary must have been after sunset on that Sabbath, aching with fresh memories of Friday afternoon, unable to look ahead to see Sunday morning's glory. Might it be that Mary of Magdala, whom so many Christians associate with repentance, discovered the true depths of her spiritual poverty in those dark moments, bereft of the gentle Man who had guided her through so many storms before?

Jesus Christ, the King of kings and Lord of lords, crucified ... dead ... and buried. Mary, Satan's former slave, had seen everything. Can any of us fully comprehend the enormity of her heart's burden? It is no coincidence that God chose this woman over all His followers to be on hand to greet His Son when, into her living death, Jesus would deliver His deathless life.

Resurrection Morning

And this is the promise that he Himself gave us, the promise of eternal life. 1 John 2:25 NEB

In the waning hours of the Sabbath following Christ's crucifixion, on the first day of the week before dawn, Mary left her nighttime lodgings and returned to the garden tomb. Joanna, Salome, James's mother, and other women — carrying spices they had prepared for anointing Jesus' body — joined her. It had not occurred to any of them that their plan to pay tribute to their Teacher would prove futile.

"Who will roll the stone away from the entrance of the tomb?" they wondered after leaving for the Lord's resting place (Mark 16:3). Securing the stone's position had been one thing. By design, that had been relatively easy. But once it had slipped into its bedrock groove, the slab's removal would require more strength than the women could muster.

The mourners fully expected to arrive at a sealed gravesite guarded by Roman soldiers. Instead, angels greeted them. At the sight of the radiantly attired heavenly beings, the guards, shaking with fright, had tumbled over in a deathlike state of paralysis.

The first angel the women saw, Matthew tells us, was sitting on the stone, away from the tomb's entrance. Understandably frightened by the sight, Mary and the others heard God's messenger tell them not to be afraid. *Jesus was alive!* (Matt. 28:2–6).

Inside the tomb, recounts Mark, the women saw a young man dressed in a white robe, seated on the sepulcher's right side. "Don't be alarmed," the angel said. "You are looking for Jesus the Nazarene, who was crucified. He has risen! He is not here. See the place where they laid him. But go, tell his disciples and Peter, 'He is going ahead of you into Galilee. There you will see him, just as he told you'" (Mark 16:5–7).

Filled with great joy, the dazed women rushed out of the tomb.

Naturally, Mary and the others began to wonder about what they had just witnessed. Then, according to Luke, they looked up and saw two more men, dressed in clothes "gleaming like lightning," suddenly standing beside them. Struck with fear, the women bowed down with their faces to the ground. Then came another amazing announcement: "Why do you look for the living among the dead? He is not here; he has risen! Remember how he told you, while he was still with you in Galilee . . ." (Luke 24:6).

Remember. . . . Had grief and doubt completely blinded them? While He was still with them, Jesus had said He must be delivered into the hands of sinful men to be crucified. He clearly told them He would be raised again on the third day. But it was not until the angels' reminder of the Lord's prophetic words that the women remembered — and trembled.

Once again, Mary of Magdala found herself in the midst of God's greatest story. A central figure at the Crucifixion, she was now the leading witness at Jesus' entombment and resurrection.

The Search

> *For God is greater than our hearts, and he knows everything.* 1 John 3:20

*Y*et, even Mary had forgotten what the Lord had said.

I saw Him die. I saw Joseph and Nicodemus wrap Him in His grave linens and lay His body in the tomb. I saw the stone-sealed tomb. I saw the sun set on Sabbath eve. I saw the darkness. . . . Is this why I didn't remember until now that this is exactly the way Jesus said it would be? Why do I still find it so hard to believe?

So much had happened so fast. As Mary told the apostles what she had seen and heard in the garden and at the tomb, she probably was not very surprised by the group's reaction to her words: *"Mary, what you're saying doesn't make any sense!"* Peter, however, got up and ran immediately to the tomb. John left with him, and Mary followed, not far behind.

Having outrun his companions, John was the first to reach the silent chamber. It was a fact: The stone had been rolled away. *But where was Jesus?* The disciple walked toward the carved-out cave and, bending over, peered inside it. There were the discarded linen strips, lying where Jesus' body should have been, just as Mary and the other women had described it. But John did not go in (John 20:5).

Simon Peter arrived next. Entering the tomb, the disciple's breathing rate and heartbeat were surely at peak levels as he stood gasping for air, his bearded face drenched in sweat after the fast dash to reach the Lord's crypt. He, too, saw the linen pieces. Then he noticed the burial cloth used to wrap Jesus' head. It had been taken off and carefully folded, separate from the other strips of fabric (John 20:6–7).

But where was Jesus? Where had they taken His body? No angels appeared to interpret the evidence this time. Finally, John joined Peter inside the tomb. Viewing the unforgettable display of evidence before him, the Lord's most beloved disciple believed the truth (John 20:8).

Heading back toward town, the two disciples must have passed Mary on their way out of the tomb as she stood outside, crying (John 20:11). While John and Peter returned home, Mary remained, keeping her lonely vigil. Overcome with emotion, the tears refused to stop as the bereaved woman continued to hunt for her Savior.

Mary was not thinking of herself that morning. Her love for Jesus had become the controlling factor in her life, and with the events of Good Friday indelibly imprinted on her mind and heart, her life could never be the same again. The cross of Christ, and her identification with it, had separated Mary of Magdala from the rest of the world.

Face-to-Face

> *How great is the love the Father has lavished on us, that we should be called children of God!* 1 John 3:1

eeking into the tomb, she heard someone speak.

"Woman, why are you crying?" the angels said. There they were, two of them, dressed in white garments, seated where Jesus' body had been — one at the head and one at the foot (John 20:12). *Why had John and Peter not seen them?*

"They have taken my Lord away," Mary answered, still weeping, "and I don't know where they have put him" (John 20:13).

As soon as she said this, she turned and saw a man standing there — the gardener, she thought — and once again, she heard the question: "Woman, why are you crying?" (John 20:14–15 NEB). The tears had drenched her dress. Her eyes were swollen from crying. She was weak with hunger and fatigue. But Mary had only one concern: to find Jesus.

"Who is it you are looking for?"

"Sir, if you have carried him away," Mary sobbed, "tell me where you have put him, and I will get him" (John 20:15). She had to find Jesus!

"Mary."

She heard Him say it. She knew His voice. *Jesus was calling her name!*

Mary swirled around and found herself face-to-face with the Lord. Turning her back to the tomb, she cried out in Aramaic, "Rabboni! (which means Teacher)" (John 20:16). Then, without thinking, she rushed forward, impelled by an irresistible desire to cling to Jesus.

"No!" her Redeemer cautioned. "Do not hold on to me, for I have not yet returned to the Father. Go instead to my brothers and tell them, 'I am returning to my Father and your Father, to my God and your God' (John 20:17).

My Father and your Father . . . my God and your God.

This was the reason Jesus had willingly submitted death on the cross. The breach was healed! And Mary of Magdala, watching, waiting, and searching during the dim hours of that seemingly endless Sabbath weekend, was the first to hear the world's Savior say it.

Carrying the News

This is love: not that we loved God, but that he loved us and sent his Son as an atoning sacrifice for our sins. 1 John 4:10

Dead . . . buried . . . and back to life again! Leaving the empty tomb far behind, Mary ran back to town with the news: *"I have seen the Lord!"* (John 20:18).

Mary of Magdala — the main witness mentioned at the Lord's tomb on Resurrection morning, the woman who lingered behind after the apostles' departure, the first person to greet Jesus after the Crucifixion — was commissioned by the Lord Himself (and earlier, by direct command of the angels) to carry the astounding announcement to His disciples. In all four gospels, Mary is the only one placed at every scene related to Jesus' crucifixion and resurrection. Her faithful witness as the primary proclaimer of Jesus' message is not to be missed. It was not just that she saw and heard these things; she was also commissioned by the Lord to tell others the news.

What an incredible testimony! Mary's story, so full of courage and commitment to God's Son, is worth remembering regularly. But let us also honor her for enduring the joyless agony of the Cross, staying with Joseph and Nicodemus as they wrapped the Lord's body, and keeping her tear-soaked watch at Jesus' tomb.

The prophet Isaiah wrote, "This is the one I esteem: he who is humble and contrite in spirit, and trembles at my word" (Isa. 66:2). For Mary, God's grace of brokenness was part of the glory of that golden Resurrection morning: The gift of contrition cleared the way for Mary's faith to find its highest joy.

Ramabai's Story

~ ❦ ~

"Thou hast touched me and I have been translated into thy peace," acknowledges Augustine in his *Confessions*. Sixteen centuries later, is this not our desire too?

The quest for spiritual truth is age-old. Every century spawns new philosophies or religions, and in recent years we have been absolutely inundated with a wide variety of mystical methods intended to expand human consciousness or unite the self with God. These are rooted in ancient beliefs and pagan practices, renamed or repackaged to appeal to modern minds.

"There is a seeking and finding that results in everlasting *life*. There is also a seeking and finding that ends in everlasting *death*. There is no neutral position,"[3] Edith Schaeffer tells us, illustrating the crucial difference between seeking to know Christ as Lord and desiring to become acquainted with Him for other reasons.

Pandita Ramabai would have probably understood what Edith Schaeffer meant. Her father, Anant Dongre, a Hindu priest, belonged to the highest caste in southern India—the Chitpawan Brahmins. A master of the Sanskrit language and teacher of the sacred Hindu scriptures, the *sastras*, he had been taught by the premier gurus in his region. The middle-aged Anant was already a forty-four-year-old widower when he took Laxmibai, the nine-year-old daughter of a Brahmin pilgrim, nine hundred miles from her home to live with him in Mangalore as his bride. Ignoring strict religious prohibitions, the defiant scholar began to teach his child-bride Sanskrit and the sacred *puranas*. It was a dangerous decision. If anyone had reported Laxmibai's study of these revered texts, she would have been immediately executed.

Realizing that his mother strongly disapproved of her daughter-in-law's taboo instruction, the Brahmin priest left his family's home and took his wife to live on a remote plateau in southern

India, where he set up an ashram in the Gungamul forest. Here, the two Hindu pilgrims studied in privacy together.

It was an odd place for an outstanding hero of the Christian faith to be born.

Sibling Wanderings

Who is it that overcomes the world? Only he who believes that Jesus is the Son of God. 1 John 5:5

*R*amabai, the Dongres' firstborn, arrived in 1858. Raised to become a Sanskrit scholar by her mother, the girl memorized 18,000 sacred Hindu verses by the time she turned twelve. Impressed by his young daughter's intellectual brilliance, Anant applied his considerable teaching skills to Ramabai's secret schooling. In time, she became familiar with nine languages, including Marathi, Kanarese, Hindustani, Bengali, and English.

Endless efforts to appease the gods through gifts and a disdain for material wealth eventually resulted in the family's severe poverty. Forced by hunger to leave their forest home, Anant and Laxmibai took their two children on a spiritual pilgrimage across India, wandering for thousands of miles on foot as they gleaned support from the offerings they received for reciting puranas. But extended temple visits and daily prayers brought no peace to Ramabai's oppressed spirit.

Many years later, Ramabai wrote, "We stayed [at the great temple at Ghatikachala] for nearly a year, but did not see a single person whose prayers were answered, not one who had not suffered much by coming there. Still we went with our service to the god."[4]

Though Ramabai's family had been warmly received by priests when they gave gifts of gold and jewelry, their poverty was continually met with nothing but indifference. When a devastating famine developed, Ramabai helplessly watched as her father grew weak and blind. She recalls how he tenderly embraced her and dedicated her life to God before succumbing to starvation: "Remember, my child, you are my youngest, my most beloved child. I have given you into the hand of our God; you are His, and to Him alone you must belong and serve Him all your life."[5]

Anant could not have foreseen where his last benediction would lead his devoted young daughter. A few months later, Ramabai's mother and older sister also wasted away and died.

Accompanied solely by her brother, Srinivasa, Ramabai took up her father's pilgrimage, walking barefoot over more than 4000 miles throughout India and sleeping under the sand along riverbanks to stay warm at night. The intelligent young woman's faith in family idols slowly eroded. "I cannot describe all the sufferings of this terrible time," she writes. "My brother and I survived and wandered about, still visiting sacred places, bathing in rivers, and worshipping the gods and goddesses in order to get our desire."

Ramabai admits the price she had to pay for spiritual purification, without any sign of the gods' blessing or approval, proved too costly. "After years of fruitless service we began to lose our faith in them," she explains.[6]

A Cluster of Trials

This is the confidence we have in approaching God: that we ask anything according to his will, he hears us. 1 John 5:14

Seeking refuge from the famine, Ramabai and Srinivasa were taken in by reform-minded Hindus in Calcutta, the *Brahmo Samaj*, who were amazed at Ramabai's remarkable talent for effortlessly composing impromptu Sanskrit poems before eager audiences. For this ability, she earned a new name — *Pandita* (Teacher), a fitting title for one who would later teach thousands of uneducated young women.

Orthodox Brahmins in the city were less impressed by her accomplishment. After charging Ramabai with undermining the integrity of Hindu families, they accused Ramabai of killing her parents and tainting sacred texts.

Estranged from her faith by this wholly undeserved mistreatment, Ramabai and her brother attended a Christian youth meeting. Having been raised in a religion that encouraged worship of colorfully painted idols and considered women of less spiritual value than cattle, Ramabai and Srinivasa found the Bible incomprehensible at first. They did not understand why Christians prayed on their knees, in silence and with their eyes closed, to a God they could not see.

As her spiritual search widened, Ramabai began to study both the Bible and Hindu scriptures. Discovering the full extent of her religion's estimate of women's value — that "women of high and low caste, as a group, were bad, very bad, worse than demons, as unholy as untruth"[7] — Ramabai launched a fervent mission of reform and resolved to spend her life raising the standards of her sisters. Soon, she became widely known for her passionate beliefs and her work on behalf of women throughout India.

In May 1880, Srinivasa died at the age of twenty-one in Calcutta, weakened by years of poverty and hunger. Six months later, Ramabai was wed to her brother's friend, Bepin Bihbari Medhavi, a lower-caste Bengali Sudra. The marriage shocked the close-knit Brahmin community. Families anticipating a more favorable match between Ramabai and one of their own sons were humiliated. As a result, Ramabai was permanently banished.

The newlyweds went to the Assam district where Ramabai's husband, a graduate of Calcutta University, began to practice law in Silchar. There, the Brahmin scholar was visited by Mr. Allan, a Baptist missionary, who taught her the central tenets of Christianity. Ramabai also found a copy of Luke's gospel in Bengali to study and, later, a Sanskrit Bible. With great happiness she welcomed her only child, a daughter named Manoramabai (Heart's Joy), into the world. Then, with no warning, crisis struck again: On February 4, 1882, after just nineteen months of marriage, Bepin contracted cholera and died.

A Mother's Burden

> *And this is the testimony: God has given us eternal life,*
> *and this life is in his Son.* 1 John 5:11

After her husband's death, Ramabai's efforts on behalf of India's oppressed women expanded. The bereaved mother's vision came into sharper focus: Twenty-three million widows —

including fifty-one thousand girls below nine years of age, according to Ramabai's estimates — were treated like prisoners of war. Their heads were shaved; they were beaten; they performed menial labor; they begged for food. People taunted and jeered at the despised girls and young women, throwing refuse instead of food into the starving widows' empty baskets. Realizing that it was her responsibility to protect Manoramabai from this terrible fate, Ramabai knew that the only way to ensure a better life for her daughter was to actively promote education and justice for all Indian women.

Traveling from place to place with her baby, Ramabai began to lecture on the benefits of women's schooling and formed chapters of the *Arya Mahila Somaj*, a society founded to help to free girls from child marriages and establish women's education-and-health programs. Defending her cause throughout India, Ramabai refused to be intimidated by the brutal tactics of her adversaries, reasoning, "Men look on women as chattels: We make every effort to deliver ourselves from this situation. But some will say this is a rebellion against man, and that to do this is sin. To leave men's evil acts unrebuked and remain unmoved before them is a great sin."[8]

One year after her husband's death, Ramabai and her daughter departed for England.

Originally, Ramabai planned to study at Cheltenham's Ladies' College in order to more effectively promote educational reform in India, but soon after her arrival, she decided to be baptized at an Anglican church. When news of the rite reached India, people were furious over what they considered to be Ramabai's betrayal of her cultural heritage. It was not the first time that Ramabai had provoked outrage with her strong-willed sense of independence. And it would not be the last.

Healed Eyes

If anyone acknowledges that Jesus is the Son of God,
God lives in him and he in God. 1 John 4:15

Ramabai's search for truth had taken her on extensive pilgrimages back and forth across India to visit Hindu temples, led her to live among Calcutta's religious elite, and now carried her on an ocean journey to reside near a British convent, where she discussed her beliefs with Anglican nuns.

Her private encounters with God were another matter. Hear Ramabai's heartfelt confession as she describes reaching the realization that self-perfection is humanly impossible:

> My eyes were being gradually opened; I was waking up to my own hopeless condition as a woman, and it was becoming clearer and clearer to me that I had no place anywhere as far as religious consolation was concerned. I became quite dissatisfied with myself.
>
> I do not know if any one of my readers has ever had the experience of being shut up in a room where there was nothing but thick darkness and then groping in it to find something of which he or she was in dire need. I can think of no one but a blind man, whose story is given in St. John, chapter nine. He was born blind and remained so for forty years of his life; and then suddenly he found the Mighty One, who could give him eyesight. Who could have described his joy at seeing the daylight, where there had not been a particle of hope of his ever seeing it?
>
> I looked to the blessed Son of God who was lifted up on the cross and there suffered death, even the death of the cross, in my stead, that I might be made free from the bondage of sin and from the fear of death, and I received life. Oh, the love, the unspeakable love of the Father for me, a lost sinner, which gave His only Son to die for me! I had not merited this love, but that was the very reason He showed it to me.
>
> How good, how indescribably good! What good news for me a woman, a woman born in India, among Brahmins who hold out no hope for me and the likes of me! The Bible declares that Christ did not reserve this great salvation for a particular caste or sex.... I had not to wait till after undergoing births and deaths for countless millions of times, when I should become a Brahmin man, in

order to get to know the Brahma. And then, was there any joy and happiness to be hoped for? No, there was nothing but to be amalgamated into Nothingness....

The Holy Spirit made it clear to me from the Word of God, that the salvation that God gives through Christ is present, and not something future. I believed it, I received it, and I was filled with joy.[9]

Like Mary of Magdala, when Ramabai heard Jesus calling her name, her life was changed forever.

Seeking and Studying

We know that we live in him and he in us, because he has given us of his Spirit. 1 John 4:13

For about a year and a half, Ramabai remained in England with her young daughter, debating various church doctrines and taking arts and science classes. Even more important, she became involved in benevolent work among the poor. It was a turning point for Ramabai, whose understanding of the Christian life now could link divine love and human service closely together.

"I began to think that there was a real difference between Hinduism and Christianity," she reflected later. "I realized, after reading the fourth chapter of St. John's Gospel, that Christ was truly the Divine Savior He claimed to be, and no one but He could transform and uplift the downtrodden womanhood of India and every land."[10] Nurtured by a fertile environment of daily prayer and Christian companionship, the seeds of Ramabai's budding faith took root as her emerging vision for ministry grew stronger.

Upon being invited to spend two weeks in the United States to visit Anandibai Joshi, the first Indian to receive her M.D. degree from the Women's Medical College in Pennsylvania, Ramabai left England for America. She ended up staying for two years while she learned new teaching methods in Philadelphia and wrote her first manuscript, *The High-Caste Hindu Woman*. Published in 1887, the book gripped the hearts of educated American women. That same year, after speaking to a full-capacity crowd in Boston, the acclaimed author founded an organization to promote education for India's child-widows — the Ramabai Association. The Board of Trustees included representatives from at least five major denominations. The next year, she sailed for Bombay from San Francisco.

In 1889, just six weeks after her arrival in India, Ramabai established her school for child-widows, *Sarada Sadan* — the House of Wisdom. Within three months, twenty-two students were enrolled at the new school.

Around the Corner

> *This is love for God: to obey his commands.*
> *And his commands are not burdensome, for everyone*
> *born of God overcomes the world.* 1 John 5:3–4

At the beginning of her educational ministry, Ramabai believed that the best way to attract students to Christ was to introduce the Gospel within a secular environment. Ramabai still gave lectures and preached in Hindu temples, but she also shared her Christian faith. The school was nonsectarian, though students were welcome to join Ramabai's "private" Bible studies for prayer and praise. Hindu scriptures were available to her students, as was the Bible. For Ramabai, modeling her Christian life publicly before her students, combined with adopting a "no open proselytizing" policy, allowed her to introduce Jesus within a hostile culture after her return from the West. The approach worked: Many students were eager to participate in their teacher's "private" morning devotions. It was not long until a number of the girls had committed their lives to Christ.

Ramabai's strategy was so successful that she was forced to leave town the next year. Due to vicious rumors and newspaper attacks about the conversions taking place at the school, it became too dangerous for her to remain in Bombay. So, in 1890, the unique evangelist left Bombay with her daughter and eighteen widows and took her ministry to Puni. Within three years, the House of Wisdom's enrollment had reached fifty-three students.

But the bitter Hindu hostility was far from over. In 1893, after a dispute with her local advisors, a number of influential members resigned from the school's Board of Directors. The removal of twenty students from the school by angry parents immediately followed. The providential blowup, however, resulted in positive changes for Ramabai's ministry: She was finally free to openly share the Gospel with the remaining widows, whose former faith community refused to grant them mercy or refuge. In November 1895, twelve students were baptized as Christians. Word of Ramabai's tender care and highly effective evangelism methods traveled quickly.

As the school in Puni was getting off the ground, Ramabai's faith, which had been largely based on rational arguments, took off in a delightfully different direction. Inspired by the biographies of other fervent Christians — George Muller, Hudson Taylor, and John Paton — Ramabai's dedication to serving the Lord deepened. Renewed by the Holy Spirit and resting in God's grace, she gained a greatly increased appreciation for Jesus' love and forgiveness. The burden of her guilt lifted. Harvest time had arrived.

Multiplied Talents

> *There is no fear in love. But perfect love drives out fear, because fear has to do with punishment. The one who fears is not made perfect in love.* 1 John 4:18

To purchase land for the expansion of her work, Ramabai tried, unsuccessfully, to cash in her life insurance policy. When her American friends discovered that Ramabai was planning to buy property and enlarge the school, they sent back word that the money was on its way. In 1896, when widespread famine struck her generation for the second time, the mission was already prepared to open its doors to additional students.

Disguised as a Hindu pilgrim, Ramabai set out to find impoverished widows and bring them back to the mission for her special brand of care. While staying at a Krishna worship center in North India at Brindaban, Ramabai was profoundly disturbed by what she witnessed. Thousands of girls and young women, whom the priests abused as temple prostitutes and later cast into the streets to endure a persecuted existence, wandered throughout the city. Gathering up as many of the homeless victims as the mission could safely support, Ramabai assembled six hundred widows and took them to her home in Puni, where she then clothed, fed, and educated the shaken survivors.

As famine swept the region, hundreds more of the homeless widows appeared at Ramabai's gate — all of them in desperate need of shelter. Temporary grass huts were built. Orchards and gardens were planted. Cattle were kept. Deep wells were dug. Fields of grain were sown. And true revival followed.

Every day, a group of girls visited Ramabai's room to pray. Many confessed their sins and renounced their worship of false gods. Countless students were converted to Christ: On one occasion, Ramabai observed seventeen cartloads of new believers being taken to be baptized in the Bheema River as their joyous choruses of praise filled the air.

At a revival meeting, Ramabai formally dedicated the mission, naming it *Mukti Sadan* (House of Salvation). The unique sanctuary also became known as a house of prayer. "Many hundreds of the girls and young women who have come to my Home ever since its doors were opened for them have found Christ as I have," Ramabai points out in her life story, *A Testimony*. "They are capable of thinking for themselves. They have had their eyes opened by reading the Word of God, and many of them have been truly converted and saved, to the praise and glory of God."

She adds: "I thank God for letting me see several hundred of my sisters, the children of my love and prayer, gloriously saved. All this was done by God in answer to the prayers of faith of thousands of His faithful servants in all lands, who are constantly praying for us all."[11]

Pressing On

> *And so we know and rely on the love*
> *God has for us.* 1 John 4:16

*B*y 1900, when another famine hit, almost 2000 people were under the mission founder's care. Of these, nearly 1,400 were girls and young women under the age of twenty.

God's plan for the mission continued to unfold. Ramabai bought twenty-two more acres from a liquor dealer located across the street from the House of Salvation, where a new building complex, the House of Mercy, sheltered single mothers, abused women, and youth offenders. Ramabai supervised the education of orphan boys, village children, and visually impaired students as well.

Dormitories, guest rooms, storage facilities, offices, and a bakery were added. As time went by, a hospital and a church were built. The indefatigable Christian worker also established income-generating businesses where people learned and used a wide variety of vocational skills, including weaving, printing, bookbinding, leatherworking, shoemaking, carpentry, and blacksmithing. The products of their labor were then sold at roadside stands to help support the mission. For these and her many other achievements, Ramabai was awarded the British Empire's highest honor by the King: the Kaiser-i-Hind gold medal.

There were also severe hardships over the years. Criticism of Ramabai's work persisted; the dirt-covered refugees carried terrible diseases; several girls set fire to mission buildings; past Brahmin acquaintances threatened destruction; cholera and bubonic plague epidemics delivered death and quarantine; famine continued; storms raged. But God had given Ramabai this verse from His Word: "No weapon forced against you will prevail" (Isa. 54:17). The faithful servant chose to cling to her Father's immutable promise.

In the final fifteen years of her life, Ramabai did another beautiful thing: She learned Hebrew and Greek and then worked on a Marathi translation of the Bible. Having dedicated everything to God, with all operations financed without bank accounts, a stable budget, or endowments, Ramabai viewed her sole personal property as "a few clothes and my Bible."

She wrote: "We are not rich, not great, but we are happy, getting our daily bread directly from the loving hands of our Heavenly Father, having not a *pice* (Indian coin) over and above our daily necessities . . . we have nothing to fear from anybody, nothing to lose, and nothing to regret. The Lord is our Inexhaustible Treasure."[12] It was a memorable testimony, indeed.

Believing that Manoramabai would succeed her in supervising the schools and missions in Puni, Ramabai was brokenhearted by her daughter's death in 1921. Though deeply grieving the loss, her acceptance of Manoramabai's passing as part of God's divine plan allowed Ramabai to continue her work with gentle strength. For two more years, she remained a living example of God's love in action — an inspiring source of wisdom to thousands of her friends, supporters, and students.

As the Bible translation neared completion, Ramabai fell gravely ill while proofreading and correcting page proofs. Praying that God would sustain her life for just ten more days, she moved forward to finish this final task. Ten days later, on April 5, 1922, after the last proof had been read, Pandita Ramabai went to sleep and quietly passed away.

The international telegram sent to her supporters soon afterward simply read: "Ramabai Promoted."

Pass me not, O gentle Savior —
Hear my humble cry!
While on others Thou art calling,
Do not pass me by.
Let me at a throne of mercy
Find a sweet relief;
Kneeling there in deep contrition —
Help my unbelief.
Trusting only in Thy merit,
Would I seek Thy face;
Heal my wounded broken spirit,
Save me by Thy grace.
Thou the spring of all my comfort,
More than life to me!
Whom have I on earth beside Thee?
Whom in heav'n but Thee?

— Fanny Crosby (1820–1915)
"Pass Me Not"

CONCLUSION

*A*ssertiveness. Achievement. Status. Success. These are common words in our contemporary vocabulary. Perhaps more than at any other time or place in history, people today expect comfort in every area of life: physically, socially, emotionally, and economically. Even on a spiritual level, millions of Americans seek comfortable solutions to life's perplexities and problems. It is far easier to sit and chant a mantra than to visit a dying widow in a nursing home.

Self-centered spirituality cannot touch people's hearts; in fact, it tends to do just the opposite. Unless our hearts are softened and made more pliable by God's love, as Mary's and Ramabai's were, we may find ourselves serving the Lord on the outside, yet maintaining an attitude of superiority on the inside. Is this why, in every saint's life, God bestows the grace of brokenness before He brings revival?

As we picture Mary standing on Calvary, and later, watching Jesus' body being prepared for burial, we cannot help but see that Resurrection Day was coming. But what was her experience in the hours before her awesome discovery at Jesus' empty tomb? In Ramabai's life, agonizing years of darkness came before heaven's dawning — the long-awaited conversion of a hungry heart yearning for eternal truth. In each case, the grace of brokenness arrived in advance of holy satisfaction.

Wherever we are, whatever our background is, whether we are old or young, single or married, Jesus wants us to know and serve Him. We are His beloved, unique in all creation, with gifts and talents entrusted to our care for God's great glory — "For we are God's workmanship, created in Christ Jesus to do good works, which God prepared in advance for us to do" (Eph. 2:10). But look also at these preceding verses: "For it is by grace you have been saved, through faith — and this not from yourselves, it is the gift of God — not by works, so that no one can boast" (Eph. 2:8–9).

Why is it so easy to doubt or forget this?

No matter how hard we try, we cannot create for ourselves what only God can give. "This is what all the work of grace aims at — an ever deeper knowledge of God, and an ever closer relationship with Him," theologian Dr. J. I. Packer reminds us in *Knowing God.* "Grace is God drawing us sinners closer and closer to Himself."

He asks, "How does God in grace prosecute this purpose? Not by shielding us from assault by the world, the flesh, and the Devil, nor by protecting us from burdensome and frustrating circumstances, nor yet by shielding us from troubles created by our own temperament and psychology; but rather by exposing us to all these things, so as to overwhelm us with a sense of our own inadequacy, and to drive us to cling to Him more closely."[13]

Remember Mary's reaction when she turned away from the tomb and recognized the gardener? After the long hours of enduring the darkness, her first reaction to seeing Jesus was to rush toward Him with outstretched arms.

When we call on the Lord with a humble heart, realizing our complete dependence upon Him, we are drawn into a divine embrace, the mysterious intimacy of a holy relationship with our risen Savior. Waiting upon Him, we grow acutely aware of our need for God. Mary and Ramabai learned how to wait on the Lord. And, with God's help, so can we — just as my friends Erin and Kathryn are learning to do.

Have you ever approached the Lord, expecting Him to judge you, only to be surrounded by His mercy and grace? Has He ever ministered His love and healing to you just when you felt you deserved His rejection?

How easy and natural it is to believe that the Lord is like an earthly parent, or a Pharisee, who will mete out the human punishment we think we deserve. But circumstances that deliver brokenness into our lives, no matter how unpleasant they may be at the moment, produce "a harvest of righteousness and peace" (Heb. 12:11), not condemnation.

We will inevitably fail in our attempts to achieve perfection. There are no loopholes in the Christian life, no detours on the walk of faith. Yet the Lord is faithful to His promises to us. Jesus loves us so much that He will accomplish our complete restoration through the process we call sanctification. He is not just out to make us whole — He is out to make us holy.

As we submit to God's unflagging efforts to change us from the inside out, our true identity is slowly but surely being conformed to the image of His Son. The secret of our success is this: *Christ in us, the hope of glory.* Although we must wait until we meet Him to receive the fullness of all that this means, our obedience to His Word, by the Holy Spirit working in our lives, brings us ever closer to this goal. And the grace of brokenness helps to get us there.

Points for Reflection

1. I am most aware of my need for the grace of brokenness when . . .
2. Even though I know that brokenness is God's gift, I sometimes struggle with accepting it as such, especially when it comes to . . .
3. Mary of Magdala's story most surprises me when she . . .
4. Brokenness in my life is easiest to accept if . . .
5. Pandita Ramabai's testimony encourages me to . . .
6. Relying on the Lord's strength requires that I . . .

Prayer: Lord, thank You for the gift of brokenness. Heavenly Father, send Your living waters; revive us by the power of Your Word. Breathe upon us, work within us, renew us by Your Holy Spirit, for Your honor and glory, now and forevermore. In Jesus' name, we pray. Amen.

~: 🍇 :~

I will exalt you, O LORD, for you lifted me
out of the depths
and did not let my enemies gloat over me.
O LORD, my God, I called to you for help
and you healed me.
O LORD, you brought me up from the grave;
you spared me from going down into the pit.
Sing to the LORD, you saints of his;
praise his holy name.
For his anger lasts only a moment,
but his favor lasts a lifetime;
weeping may remain for a night,
but rejoicing comes in the morning.

—Psalm 30:1–5

What! Lean upon yourself? Count on your works?

Could self-love, pride and perversity have a more miserable fruit?

It is to deliver them from this that God makes all chosen souls pass through a fearful time of poverty, misery and nothingness.

He desires to destroy in them gradually all the help and confidence they derive from themselves so that he may be their sole source of support, their confidence, their hope, their only resource.[14]

— Jean-Pierre de Caussade (1675–1751)

Chapter Two

Belief

~: 🍇 :~

Faith is the root of all blessings. Believe, and you shall
be saved; believe, and you must needs be satisfied;
believe, and you cannot but be comforted and happy.[1]
— Jeremy Taylor (1613–1667)

*G*od creates out of nothing," the Swedish philosopher Søren
Kierkegaard noted a century ago, "but He does what is still
more wonderful: He makes saints out of sinners."

Our Good Shepherd diligently searches for those who stray
from His tender care, regardless of how desolate or dangerous
their terrain becomes. No matter what we have done or how
unclean we may feel inside, Jesus is waiting for us to walk with
Him. He will not condone what we have done, but He will not
condemn us. Instead, He calls us to leave our old life behind and
walk with Him into the light of eternity.

The grace of belief, the gift of faith birthed in our hearts by
the Holy Spirit, helps to keep us from ignoring our boundary
lines.

Belief shows us that goodness and mercy will follow us every
day of our lives, revealing the way ahead, calming our trembling
spirits, and straightening our distorted thinking. Without belief,
we become vulnerable to all manner of attack; with it, we are pro-
tected from trouble, surrounded by songs of deliverance, in a hiding place where no enemy may effectively assail us (Ps. 32:7).
Though the means by which God sends this grace differs from
person to person — it may arrive early or late in life, after decades
of questioning or with little searching, before the formation of

47

harmful habits or long past childhood's closing — the results of true Christian belief lead us to a common end: eternal salvation.

For my friend's daughter Laurie, belief came when she was least expecting it. Estranged from her affluent family, addicted to amphetamines, and pregnant with her boyfriend's baby, she turned to her parents for help. They immediately counseled her to keep the baby and supplied the support she needed to stop using "speed" while insisting on daily urine testing and enforcing other restrictions after Laurie's return.

Motivated by her desire to have a healthy baby, Laurie simultaneously kicked her drug habit and quit smoking. In the course of time, she also committed herself to Christ. "The baby may have saved Laurie's life," observes her father, Neil, an Atlanta-area businessman.

"Our entire family was affected during those early months of her pregnancy and recovery. After more than ten years away from church, one at a time, we all started attending again. As the months rolled by, I saw my daughter come alive," he explains thoughtfully. "It was as if the Laurie we had known before her encounter with drugs 'returned' to us."

My friend Carol distinctly remembers how the grace of belief changed her life. When she was in her mid-twenties, she seriously contemplated suicide after her abortion and subsequent breakup with the baby's father. "Without Jesus, I felt there was no future for me. None whatsoever. I completely lacked the motivation to turn my situation around, and did not have the power to heal my mind or heart. But God gave me a fresh start," Carol shares openly.

Smiling, she says, "I believe Jesus has made me a new creation, and as the years go by, this incredible truth becomes more real to me every day."

I became acquainted with Carol shortly after she became a Christian and remember reacting with disbelief as she recounted what her life had been like earlier. She is a powerful example to me of what it means to be "transformed by grace."

Though the lingering aftereffects of her former lifestyle persist, her identity is no longer shaped by them. "It took me a while to figure out that just because I believed in Jesus that it didn't mean that the pain of the past had been erased all of a sudden. My past continues to play a part in my life," admits Carol, pausing for a moment. "I still attend weekly recovery group meetings, and occasionally face guilt feelings or grieve over the baby I lost. But my former ordeals aren't the dominant theme of my life. Believing that God has forgiven me helps me to forgive myself."

Unlike Carol, my friend Tricia began following Christ when she was a teenager. Home Bible studies and worship services took up much of her free time, giving Tricia an out-of-the-mainstream reputation with her high school peers. After graduation, she attended a nearby university and worked in a teen guidance clinic before getting married and becoming a mother of two children.

For many years, Tricia remained an active, vibrant Christian. But the crisis of divorce from an unfaithful spouse changed the quality of her commitment. My friend no longer felt comfortable going to church, so she quit going — for the first time since she had become a Christian. Tricia's social circle widened to include companions who offered solace without judgment. They also pulled her away from God. Soon, Tricia found herself engaging in many of the activities she had considered off-limits in adolescence, and began to question her belief. Eventually, she decided to stop following Christ.

For a number of years, Tricia wandered through an agonizing wasteland. But when memories of childhood sexual abuse came into clearer focus, she got the help she needed to face past horrors.

I grieve over what my friend has been through over her lifetime. More than anything, I want her to realize that nothing can separate her from God's love: The Lamb whom she once called Lord longs for her return to safe pasture.

I do not know for certain what I would have done in Tricia's position. How can any of us know?

When our troubles trap us and threaten to defeat us, we can ask the Lord to reaffirm our belief in His strong presence as we wait upon Him, in all of our undeniable weakness, to renew our strength.

Accepting belief as a divine grace helps us to realize that faith does not originate with us: It is a gift that comes from God. As in the story of Rahab, belief often appears in the most unlikely places, with little or no warning, where few can fully comprehend its far-reaching wonder, whether we are "open" to receive it or not. Who, for example, would have ever thought that the Lord would grant belief to a Jericho prostitute on the eve of her doomed city's downfall?

Rahab's Story

*n ancient Jericho, the fortified Canaanite oasis located in
the heart of the Holy Land, a small inn sits perched atop a
gap of twelve to fifteen feet between a double-walled embankment
ringing the city. Visible to potential customers for miles beyond
the main gates, the popular house is a prime piece of real estate,
providing easy access to a colorful retinue of local clients and foreign visitors. Here, exotic entertainment promises each patron a
private evening of enjoyment at the end of a hectic day. Run by
an enterprising businesswoman with a reliable reputation, it is a
sumptuous spot offering exquisite food, fine linens, and flickering
candlelight, where the sights and smells melt together to form an
intoxicating blend of Middle Eastern delights — the owner's distinctive trademark.

A night's lodging at this hardworking harlot's house of pleasure is expensive, but to Rahab's man of the hour, any sum seems
worth the price. Over the years, the sophisticated survivor has
seen and heard it all, listened to a thousand stories with perfect
discretion, as sheiks and soldiers alike have passed swiftly through
her door. Rahab is wise and she is weary.

There must be something more.

Her independence from the usual restrictions placed on
women, at least in the beginning, brought freedom from the con-
fining social customs associated with marriage. Having made the
most of her public position among powerful men, Rahab is an
accomplished artisan, a self-employed entrepreneur accustomed
to calling her own shots, who has learned to ignore taunting jeers
and curious glances. But she has started to avoid the places where
mothers and babies gather. Seeing them makes her feel too angry
and alone.

Her heart, like a chunk of dry ice, burns steadily below freezing. The stifled ache threatens to break up the numb, hard center of her arctic soul.

Change of Climate

Now faith is being sure of what we hope for and
certain of what we do not see. Hebrews 11:1

$\mathcal{O}$ne day, without blinking, Rahab casts a discerning eye on two new guests as they walk through her front door. She notices they seem unimpressed by their sensual surroundings.

After the usual pleasantries are exchanged, it is immediately evident these men are different from her usual customers. Natives of Shittim, they show no interest in buying Rahab's services and tell her that they are Hebrew spies on a mission from God. The seasoned scouts soberly inform her that the city of Jericho is doomed; their words sound extreme, outlandish, harsh. Yet something about the two solemn men suggests to Rahab they are worth trusting.

Under other circumstances, the disillusioned harlot would be skeptical, laugh, and throw them out. There simply was not enough time in her day to waste even one second listening to a couple of grim-faced pilgrims carry on about religious prophecies and morbid speculations. But Rahab invites the men to stay for dinner. For some strange reason she cannot explain, their words ring true.

Perhaps it is because she has grown tired of Jericho's gods. She has heard of the priests' cruel hypocrisies from reliable sources, and pities their slavelike crew of ritual prostitutes who, mistakenly, believe in the sanctity of their service. Rahab knows better: The women's labor generates a steady stream of gold that flows straight into the temple treasury. In Rahab's opinion, the pagan gods of Canaan are capable only of silence — they are statues made of stone and sweat, and that is all. Besides, what good have any of these worthless idols ever done for her?

Point of No Return

But we are not of those who shrink back and are destroyed,
but of those who believe and are saved. Hebrews 10:39

s the day wears on, Rahab reflects upon what Joshua's spies have said. Her extensive contact with travelers from throughout the region has afforded her familiarity with Hebrew history. She already knows, for example, how the slaves were freed under Moses' leadership in Egypt. She has heard incredible accounts about the supernatural parting of the Red Sea and was told the devastating details concerning the total destruction of the Amorites to the east of the Jordan River.

What kind of God could possibly be capable of such power?

Thinking over these facts, Rahab considers her risks in the same way she calculates her monthly business expenses: *If what the spies say is true, and I help them, they may, in turn, help me ... but if the king finds out about the attempted cover-up, he will put me in prison for treason, or worse ... on the other hand, if I turn the Hebrews over to the local authorities, business will undoubtedly benefit from my proven loyalty ... yet, if the town is about to be destroyed by the Israelites, my allegiance to a Canaan ruler no longer matters....*

"Before God can deliver us," Augustine observed, "we must undeceive ourselves." With a canny kind of clearheadedness, Rahab draws closer to her deliverance as she weighs her chances and selects a course of action. Telling the spies they must hide quickly, she asks them to follow as she silently slips upstairs, climbs through a little door in the ceiling, and steps onto the sun-baked roof.

Soon, a knock at the front door convinces Rahab she has made the right decision. It is a message from the king of Jericho: "Bring out the men who came to you and entered your house, because they have come to spy out the whole land" (Josh. 2:3).

In an instant, Rahab realizes what she must do.

"Yes, the men came to me, but I did not know where they had come from," she lies, choosing each word with caution. "At dusk, when it was time to close the city gate, the men left. I don't know which way they went. Go after them quickly. You may catch up with them" (Josh. 2:4–5). The soldiers standing in the foyer do not doubt the woman, nor do they demand to search her house. Instead, they do as she says — a telling indicator of Rahab's esteemed position within the royal household and Jericho's military community.

Rooftop Revelations

> *By faith we understand that the universe was formed at God's command, so that what is seen was not made out of what was visible.* Hebrews 11:3

*I*t may be that Rahab did not consider her options ahead of time, that it was not until the soldiers were actually standing on her doorstep that she was certain of her choice. When did the Lord reveal the truth to her? And at what point did she choose to believe it?

For Rahab, the mysterious process of conversion appears to have happened in the same way it does for each of us. According to His timing, when the moment was exactly right, the Lord placed His mighty hand upon His daughter, planted faith deep within her hurting heart, and with absolute authority and irresistible loving-kindness, called her home.

Hear her words, inspired by the Spirit, as she sits up on the rooftop with Joshua's spies later that evening: "I know that the LORD has given this land to you and that a great fear of you has fallen on us, so that all who live in this country are melting in fear because of you. . . . your God is God in heaven above and on the earth below" (Josh. 2:9, 11). Rahab's stunning confession of faith, coupled with her positive affirmation of Israel's imminent victory, is astounding — a divinely inspired proclamation for Joshua's men to carry back to their commander-in-chief.

We can only imagine what went through the spies' minds when they realized God was using this particular woman — a well-known Canaanite prostitute — to supply strong hope to Hebrew warriors. With stars glimmering overhead, the stalwart trio of unlikely heroes, gazing up at the heavens from a makeshift hideaway on a Jericho rooftop, cooperate with God in creating history.

A freshening breeze brings a cool night's respite to the swel-tering city, accompanied by an unseen wind carrying truth to Rahab's mind, igniting her spirit with the healing heat of God's unfailing love. Lifted by the Creator's unchanging will from the shame and social confinement of her notorious harlotry, Rahab's humiliating legacy is exchanged without warning for a unique position of honor, bringing a crisp awareness of her humble appointment.

The Scarlet Signal

So do not throw away your confidence; it will
be richly rewarded. Hebrews 10:35

new bravery transforms Rahab's callous chutzpah into con-cerned compassion. Reminded of her loved ones, she is moved to petition the concealed spies to spare her family first and, sensing that the timing is right, instantly proposes a pact.

"Now then, please swear to me by the LORD that you will show kindness to my family, because I have shown kindness to you," she pressures Joshua's men boldly. "Give me a sure sign that you will spare the lives of my father and mother, my brothers and sisters, and all who belong to them, and that you will save us from death" (Josh. 2:12–13).

"Our lives for your lives!" the infiltrators vow, ignoring the worldly woman's obvious liabilities. Then they outline the terms of their agreement with an irrevocable promise: "If you don't tell what we are doing, we will treat you kindly and faithfully when the LORD gives us the land" (Josh. 12:14).

Many men lavishly rewarded Rahab before, but nothing com-pares with this: Among Jericho's citizens, only Rahab and her family are to be spared by Joshua's advancing army. And beyond that? Whatever happens, Rahab feels certain that the Hebrews' living God will not desert her.

Before helping the men to escape down a rope through an open window in the city wall, the anxious mistress of the house, who is well-acquainted with Canaan's usual military routes and prescribed conduct of maneuvers, tells the spies to hide in the hills surrounding the city for three days before rejoining Joshua's forces. As they leave, the men give Rahab a set of strict instructions. "This oath you made us swear will not be binding on us," they warn her explicitly, "unless, when we enter the land, you have tied this scarlet cord in the window through which you let us down" (Josh. 12:17–18). They also warn Rahab that she must keep her family within the house at all times to avoid their being killed in the upcoming attack on the city.

After she agrees to the spies' final terms, the subdued woman silently stands by as the two men climb down the rugged wall, keeping a steady watch until they vanish into the darkness. She then fastens the designated marker at the side of the window. Turning to go downstairs, Rahab notices that the lifeline is dyed with a blood-colored pigment and contemplates the meaning of the scarlet signal.

Many years later, the first followers of Jesus will celebrate the Passover-like symbolism of her emblem of deliverance as yet another prophetic reminder of the Lord's provision of atonement on Calvary's cross.

Last-Minute Mission

You need to persevere so that when you have done the will of God, you will receive what he has promised. Hebrews 10:36

The days following the spies' departure pass by in a blur of frenzied activity as Rahab gets ready to inform her family of Jericho's forthcoming fate and makes arrangements to care for the sizable clan during the siege. Convincing the entire group to accompany her to her home — which, to them, has always seemed to be a forbidding palace of fornication — will be no small feat. The newly established believer must first conquer her fear of treading less than lightly on her parent's generosity and goodwill.

Rahab's parents have spoken few words to their daughter in recent years. Her rough occupation is a source of ongoing anguish to her mother and father; her brothers are particularly embarrassed by their sister's work. Instead of giving them grandchildren and nieces and nephews, Rahab has brought the sharp sting of humiliation. But now, there is a way she can repay them.

"God above, be with me as I go," she petitions the Lord, still unsure of the right words to say. "Please, make a way for me, and give me an open door. . . ." Knocking on the familiar rough-hewn plank above the wooden handle, Rahab takes a deep breath and waits for the reply.

Seconds later, her estranged mother and father are standing speechless in the entryway. They immediately notice that something about Rahab's face appears changed. Is it her eyes, perhaps? Where there was previously a deadened coldness, there are now fiery sparks of radiant warmth, the unmistakable presence of an enlivening, vibrant energy. Although they are not sure why, the stunned parents are willing to listen to what their prodigal daughter has to say.

With words of peace and reconciliation, the repentant woman urgently conveys what she knows about Joshua's impending attack and Jericho's inevitable ruin, convinces her family to pack up a few of their favorite belongings, and helps them to move into her spacious inn. Then, she waits.

Saved by Faith

This is what the ancients were commended for. Hebrews 11:2

After hiding in the hills for three days as Rahab instructed, the two men safely return to camp and tell Joshua the startling news of their encounter. "The LORD has surely given the whole land into our hands," the spies report, "all the people are melting in fear because of us" (Josh. 2:24). The prostitute's illuminating words are precisely what Joshua had been waiting to hear.

Early the next morning, the Hebrew leader and all the Israelites set out from Shittim and establish their camp near the Jordan River, the watery border of the promised land, in preparation for battle. For Rahab, the brief span of time between the spies' departure and Jericho's demise is a period of testing. Because her family is residing with her, she is legitimately able to decline business offers, and in this way, her previous way of life begins to fade into the background of her days.

Yet, all around her, there are continual reminders of wasted years spent with a startling variety of men, and her family's presence, given their own discomfort with her former profession, is a mixed blessing. A woman caught between two worlds, Rahab is more than willing to discard her old self but lacks any credible evidence concerning the existence of the new person she passionately desires to become. No one can understand what is happening inside of her heart.

Gazing out her windows, she views neighbors and passersby whom she knows will soon face a violent death. Surrounded by the worship of pagan gods, all Rahab has to go by is a fleeting encounter, a strangely wonderful conversation with two mysterious men that took place weeks ago under a flickering field of stars. Even so, it is enough.

Convinced that what happened that night was real, she steadfastly refuses to remove the scarlet rope from the side of the window where the men escaped and manages to keep her family together as tension mounts within the city. A few days ago, there was news about the Israelites crossing the Jordan as the river water inexplicably parted — just as the Red Sea had dried up before Moses years ago. More recently, Rahab has received word that tens of thousands of heavily armed Hebrews are camped nearby. The city gates have been locked, food is running short, panic is widespread, and her parents' doubts are multiplying.

Still, Rahab waits.

Falling Walls

> *Therefore, since we are receiving a kingdom that*
> *cannot be shaken, let us be thankful, and so worship*
> *God acceptably, with reverence and awe.* Hebrews 12:28

What Rahab does not know is this: God is moving within Joshua's camp. He has already delivered Jericho into the hands of the Israelites and given them detailed marching instructions.

Imagine what these final days of the blockade are like for Rahab. There is no twenty-four-hour cable news network providing constant live video feeds from Joshua's camp, no daily newspaper updates, no radio broadcasts, and no telephone access. To be saved from destruction, she must wait inside a stifling house without air-conditioning, electricity, or running water, wondering if the spies' promise will be kept, listening to her distressed family's continual complaining.

Let us be honest here. Rahab has no experience with Hebrew religious rituals, possesses very limited knowledge of Jewish history, has no idea of what it means to be a descendant of Abraham, Isaac, and Jacob, and does not have a clue about what her life will soon be like. She cannot quite comprehend what is happening as she waits, staying active in her stone house, caring for all of her relatives, and watches an odd assembly of strange priests and 40,000 armed men passing under her window each day.

It gets worse. On the seventh day, the ominous sound of rams' horns fills the scorching desert air, followed immediately by the ear-splitting shriek of an entire nation's declaration of war. All around Rahab's house, there is a sudden rumbling. Some of her family are screaming as they cover their eyes; the brave ones strain to get a glimpse out the windows. With a terrifying cracking noise, the great stone walls crumble and collapse, crashing to the ground. The earth shudders. A blinding cloud of heavy dust and soot rises from the rubble, abruptly choking Rahab and her housemates. And then, Joshua and his army advance to destroy every living thing inside the city.

Rahab's Release

Let us hold unswervingly to the hope we profess,
for he who promised is faithful. Hebrews 10:23

*R*eminding her family of the Hebrew spies' oath, Rahab restrains her relatives from running into the street when they realize the extent of the holocaust's horror. The evidence of Jericho's annihilation is all around them. Every single inhabitant, except for Rahab and her family, is killed in the ensuing bloodbath.

I only need to keep them with me for a little while, and then the men will surely come to save us, Rahab keeps repeating to herself. *God in heaven, help me to believe it! Give me strength, God! I fear my family will not stay here for much longer.*

Rahab knows what to do. Pointing out that the scarlet rope still hangs from the window and that the house has not collapsed in spite of its proximity to the wall, the courageous woman tells her assembled loved ones that God will not fail them. Once again, her family believes her, just as they did before. No one leaves the inn.

Soldiers kill nearby residents on every side; the sound of squealing animals announces additional slaughter. Like a horrific nightmare, the carnage seems to take place outside of time, a seemingly endless spasm of inescapable, indescribable terror. Then, without warning, a strange quietness falls upon the neighborhood.

It is over. Rahab and her clan are safe.

A short time later, the spies arrive at the familiar house to rescue its shaken occupants. Several are in a state of shock. Others refuse to believe that they are not going to die. Following Rahab and the two Israelites, they make their way over the rocky pile of debris that was once a mighty wall and walk to a place near Joshua's camp as what is left of the city burns behind them. The appointed destruction of Jericho is complete — with one notable exception: Rahab, a former prostitute, and her entire family are alive.

Of all Jericho's citizens, only this chosen woman has been granted enough faith to believe in the one, true, everlasting God.

Pelagia's Story

~: 🍇 :~

*I*n the third century, during the reign of the Roman Emperor Numerianus, a wealthy actress named Pelagia resided in the ancient city of Antioch. Renowned for her incomparable appearance and passionate love of luxury — especially expensive clothing, unusual cosmetics, and valuable jewels — the dazzling courtesan attracted countless rich lovers.

Given her unrivaled beauty and success, Pelagia probably found it easy to seduce any man she wanted. More than likely, she found the game amusing as well as profitable. In those days, no man in Antioch, once selected for the privilege of sharing Pelagia's bed, had been known to resist her amorous advances, and no woman possessed greater allure than the renowned courtesan. One flash of her sexy smile, and the willing victim was hopelessly lost. Many men squandered their fortunes — and some actually risked their lives — attempting to win the stunning woman's admiration and affection.

Yet this mattered little to the pampered Pelagia: She valued her property and possessions much more.

Boldly riding down the city streets in her carriage, Pelagia ignored scandal and found considerable pleasure in drawing attention to herself. Flawless skin, perfect breasts, enchanting eyes, all expertly enhanced by the courtesan's artful application of the best beauty treatments available, combined to create her goddess-like status. People worshiped Pelagia for her physical attractiveness, just as movie stars and supermodels are idolized in our culture today. Adorned with fine fabrics, and catered to by various servants, the glamorous beauty would have easily qualified for *Vogue*'s front cover.

But what about refinements made upon Pelagia's neglected spirit? "Inordinate love of the flesh is cruelty," noted Bernard of

Clairvaux, a wise monk considered by many to be the last of the church Fathers, in the twelfth century, "because under the appearance of pleasing the body we kill the soul."

Long overlooked, the interior of Pelagia's soul was devoid of light, a decaying place steeped in suffocating secrecy. Her single-minded pursuit of fame and fortune, steadily reinforced by spiritually lethal rewards, had resulted in a self-loving stupor. Alienated from God and unaware of her true poverty, the courtesan's bliss became demoniacal bondage.

Then God took pity on Pelagia's enslaved spirit and, knowing in advance how much she would someday accomplish for the kingdom of heaven, tenderly proceeded to set the prisoner free.

The Decontaminated Dove

> *Nothing in all creation is hidden from God's sight. Everything is uncovered and laid bare before the eyes of him to whom we must give account.* Hebrews 4:13

Here is how it happened. One day, at the Church of St. Julian in Antioch, a virtuous bishop named Nonnos stood outside preaching a sermon to a small group of believers when Pelagia, riding by in her distinctive carriage, suddenly captured his listeners' attention. Covered with sparkling gemstones and soaked in heavily-scented musk, the famous actress's appearance shocked the pious men. Stunned by the sight, they turned their eyes to the ground.

Bishop Nonnos, on the other hand, did not act as hastily. Understanding that a more merciful response might be beneficial, Nonnos gazed with compassion at Pelagia and started to weep loudly. Soaking his garments with tears, the humbled bishop viewed the passing woman's extravagantly designed adornments as evidence of his own condemnation.

And so it was that Pelagia, having spent all of her time, money, and energy on enhancing her beauty and career, convicted this holy man of his own failure to serve God more wholeheartedly.

Speaking to the bystanders gathered around him, the bishop declared, "Woe and alas unto us, the negligent and useless ones, because we shall be ashamed during the hour of judgment by this harlot who, to please mortal men, diligently adorns herself, so she might enjoy a little but bitter pleasure. We, the mindless ones, indifferently dismiss, without regard, the soul, instead of preferring the immortal and living God. Moreover, we prefer what is vain and perishable, thus insulting and disdaining our dignity. Whereupon, we suffer loss of that wonderful and ineffable delight of perpetual blessedness."[2] After speaking for a while longer, Nonnos retired to his private cell to pray, calling out to God through his tears.

"O Most High and very compassionate One," he began, "pardon my negligence; for one day of that harlot's diligence surpasses the attempt of all my life to adorn my soul as a habitation for Thee. What excuse, therefore, shall I find before Thee, Who knows all the secrets of my heart?

"Woe is me, the wretched one! I am unworthy to enter Thy Holy Altar and am not adorned according to Thy will. Nonetheless, O Lord, do not condemn me in that day of examination, because I am desolate of every virtue and have not kept even one of Thy commandments."[3]

Upon finishing this petition, spoken by the bishop within hearing distance of his subordinate, the deacon Iacovos, Nonnos beheld a vision. While celebrating the liturgy in the temple, he saw a foul-smelling dove, muddied with dirt, flying about him. Though the stench was highly distracting, Nonnos continued with the liturgy as the bird rested on its perch close by. When the bishop reached the part of the service when the rite of baptism is ordinarily performed, the dove flew immediately toward Nonnos; extending his hand, he immersed the poor creature in the font's refreshing water.

The dove, instantly cleansed, emerged from the healing well without a spot and, sweeping upward, ascended so high that the bishop could no longer see the mysterious bird.

The next morning, Nonnos shared the vision with Iacovos before the two men joined their Christian brothers at the church. Placing a special blessing on the bishop, the head priest commissioned Nonnos to share the Gospel with the people by the Holy Spirit's grace.

In the attentive crowd, a woman named Pelagia stood close by, silently listening.

Daybreak

> *For we do not have a high priest who is unable to sympathize with our weaknesses, but we have one who has been tempted in every way, just as we are — yet was without sin.* Hebrews 4:15

The courtesan was not seeking spiritual truth. She had never gone to church before. No previous experience had prepared Pelagia to understand what the bishop was talking about as he spoke about the soul's immortality and God's righteousness.

So why was she there?

A few hours later, the actress discovered the reason for her atypical eavesdropping. As a voiceless cry erupted from deep inside her heart, something broke within Pelagia's imprisoned spirit. Weeping bitterly, she could feel the searing pain of her separation from God for the first time and ached with a godly sorrow over acts she had always believed were acceptable and amusing. It was as if she was seeing herself accurately for the first time, the person she had always been, held up and magnified for close-up examination, in contrast with the woman she suddenly desired to become. Despising the past, the repentant woman realized that she was also powerless to change it.

Straining to break free from the condemning legacy of her life, painful memories assailed Pelagia's mind as her chief enemy struggled to hang onto his former possession. But it was too late. A compelling tenderness wrapped her wounds; a comforting peace embraced her tormented being. The Lord surrounded the contrite woman with a love so great, so real, and so perfect that she never forgot the experience.

Pouring out her grief, Pelagia placed herself at the foot of the cross, and remained there for the balance of her life. Kneeling before the only Man she could not conquer, the famous courtesan privately committed her life to the Lord Jesus Christ, her truest Lover.

When the weeping subsided, Pelagia asked two of her menservants to follow the bishop and find out where he lived. Once this had been done, she wrote Nonnos a short letter. "I have heard, O saint of God, from a certain Christian," it read, "that the Master came not 'to call the righteous, but sinners to repentance' (Matt. 9:13); and that He does not despise even loathsome harlots, thieves, and tax collectors. Much rather, He, Whom the Cherubim dare not gaze upon, associated and conversed with them." The argument, compelling in its perceptive truth, arose from the living wellspring of Pelagia's awakened soul.

"If, therefore, thou art also the servant and athlete of such a Teacher," the letter continued, "show forth unto me this work. Do not loathe me as the harlot who is, as thee, of the same race and a fellow-slave. Instead, vouchsafe me, I entreat thee, to confess my sins to thee that I may save my soul. . . ."[4]

Pelagia refused to remain in the darkness any longer.

The Bishop's Response

> *Let us draw near to God with a sincere heart*
> *in full assurance of faith, having our hearts sprinkled*
> *to cleanse us from a guilty conscience and having our*
> *bodies washed with pure water.* Hebrews 10:22

Upon reading Pelagia's earnest letter, Nonnos realized that it would be unwise to meet with her alone and instructed the converted courtesan to meet him at the church to share her confession before the other church leaders.

Rejoicing at this counsel, Pelagia seized the moment and proceeded directly to the church. She bowed to the ground at the bishop's feet, washing them with her tears, and crying out in a great voice, she pleaded, "Take compassion, O holy father, and imitate thy Master. Baptize me and guide me unto repentance, because I am a sea of iniquity, an abyss of destruction, and the devil's snare and spoil; for by reason of me, many have gone to damnation. Now, by the grace of God, I regret my harlotry and seek repentance, so I might not be condemned eternally."[5]

The transformed heart of the broken woman was immediately evident to Nonnos and his Christian brothers. Giving thanks at the sight of her repentance, yet uneasy with her prostrate demonstration of contrition, they felt compelled to physically lift Pelagia from her flat-on-the-floor posture. Then Nonnos spoke to her directly. Informing the penitent woman of the prerequisites for baptism, he asked her to produce clear evidence that she had no plans to return to her previous lifestyle.

When Pelagia heard this, she again fell to the ground, wailing and weeping. "May my sins hang upon my neck. And may thou give a word at the hour of judgment, if thou dost delay and not baptize me as quickly as possible," the prone woman responded. "I desire to receive spiritual rebirth that I might be presented to the pure Bridegroom of Christ as a pure and blameless Bride. . . . I fear that, if I delay receiving Baptism, the supplanter [the Devil] shall ensnare me again and cast me into my former wanton behavior."[6] Giving God the glory for Pelagia's unwavering determination, Nonnos inquired about her name and found a spiritual sponsor, or godmother, for the new believer — a devout deaconess, the nun Romana.

Upon Pelagia's conversion and baptism, celebration spontaneously broke out around Antioch as Christians across the city praised God for the courtesan's salvation with each person counting Pelagia's happiness as his own.

Resisting Temptation

> *Therefore, since we have a great high priest who has gone through the heavens, Jesus the Son of God, let us hold firmly to the faith we profess.* Hebrews 4:14

Consider that the devil does not sleep," Angela Merici observed in the fifteenth century, "but seeks our ruin in a thousand ways."[7] Thus it is not surprising that the Devil, who understandably despised Pelagia's radical repentance, refused to go down without a fight.

Unable to wait even a minute longer, the Enemy assumed a man's appearance and started shouting and holding his head right in the midst of the baptismal service, defying the bishop, and accusing Pelagia of faithless treachery. But the new convert remained cleansed, and as she made the sign of the cross, the Devil disappeared.

That night, he visited her again. This time, the desperate fiend entered Pelagia's bedroom, where she was staying with her god-mother, and woke her up. Whispering honeyed words, he tried to seduce his former prey by promising to supply her with far greater wealth and beauty than before. Again, Pelagia defied the demon's advances. Rising from her bed, she made the sign of the cross once more, and cast the Devil out with supernatural author-ity. When she related the details of the cunning late-night temp-tation to her spiritual advisor, Romana encouraged Pelagia to remain strong and not be shaken or surprised if additional schemes assailed her.

Within days of her baptism, the rapidly reforming believer dealt another well-placed blow to the Enemy: She decided to sell all of her possessions and give the proceeds to Nonnos to be used at his discretion. Led by the Holy Spirit to take action, Pelagia sent for her most trusted slave, and requested that a detailed inventory be made of her estate. Bidding the slave to deliver the list to her at once, Pelagia submitted it to the bishop, and asked him to accept the sum of her belongings as an offering to God. "Distribute the goods as thou dost seem fit," she beseeched him, "because for me the ultimate wealth is my Bridegroom, the Mas-ter Christ."[8]

Nonnos deposited the vast treasure with the warden in charge of charitable distributions, and advised him not to withhold any-thing for the church but to give it all away to widows, orphans, and the poor. While this was being done, Pelagia took yet another exciting step of faith. Liberating her slaves, she gave each a mon-etary gift, and entreated them to seek the salvation from eternal captivity Christ freely makes available to all.

A Last Visit

Let us fix our eyes on Jesus, the author and perfecter of our faith, who for the joy set before him endured the cross, scorning its shame, and sat down at the right hand of the throne of God. Hebrews 12:2

Pelagia initially refused to eat anything that had been bought with funds obtained before her conversion, and after her baptism was fed by Romana for a brief time. On the eighth evening after Nonnos performed the holy rite, Pelagia discarded her extravagant attire and assumed the stark wardrobe of a pauper — a hair shirt covered by a tattered tunic. And then, without warning, she vanished.

Not even Romana knew where Pelagia had gone. Lamenting the loss of her exceptional disciple, the godmother was consoled by her friend the Bishop Nonnos, to whom the Holy Spirit had already revealed his beloved convert's intended hiding place. Gently reminding the grief-stricken nun of the Lord's blessing upon Mary of Bethany, he consoled the deaconess by telling her that Pelagia, like that extraordinary woman, had also chosen the good portion.

After leaving Antioch, Pelagia traveled to the Mount of Olives in Jerusalem, where she lived in seclusion for three years. Disguising herself as a man, she remained unrecognized in the community and was known only as Pelagios.

During this time, she grew in virtue and wrestled with the Enemy on numerous occasions, defeating the Devil in Christ's name every time. But God was not willing to have the cloistered woman's outstanding conquests remain hidden. At the Holy Spirit's urging, Iacovos began to yearn for worship at the Holy Sepulchre. When the deacon sought his bishop's permission to depart for Jerusalem, Nonnos granted his blessing upon the endeavor and urged Iacovos to inquire about a monk there, the Eunuch Pelagios, saying it is "because he is a consummate friend of our Lord." The bishop also told Iacovos that he would greatly benefit from visiting the holy hermit.

Not knowing that Nonnos was referring to Pelagia, the bishop's assistant made queries about the "eunuch" upon arriving in the Holy Land, and was directed to a small cell on the Mount of Olives.

A peculiar person whom Iacovos did not recognize answered the door, though the former courtesan, masked by the dual disguise of prolonged hardship and rough monk's garb, knew it was the bishop's assistant. To the deacon, the reclusive stranger was a shocking sight. Pelagia's beautiful face and voluptuous figure were gone, traded for the withered features of a true ascetic. The lovely locks, once widely known for their abundant waves, had been shorn. A holy man's attire replaced her fancy gowns. Extreme poverty and continual fasting, having slowly sculptured a serene countenance of calm repose, had erased the desirable features that previously excited the passion of Antioch's most powerful men.

As she looked from the doorway of her cell at Iacovos, Pelagia asked him if he was the assistant of the Bishop Nonnos. After he replied affirmatively, the diminutive disguised woman said only this: "Verily the man is an apostle of God. Say unto him to entreat God on behalf of my sins."[9] Then she shut the door.

The words deeply impressed Iacovos with their solemn simplicity. As he prepared to leave, Iacovos heard the monk begin to chant according to his religious order's custom. Greatly touched by Pelagios's piety, the deacon then went to sojourn with his Christian brothers living in the vicinity, where all of the priests extolled Father Pelagios as a saintly monk not lacking any virtue.

A short time after Iacovos's visit, Pelagia passed from this life into the next, and left to be with the Lord. Christians from across the area — from Jerusalem, Jordan, Jericho, and beyond — gathered for the good monk's burial. But before her body was laid to rest, the blessed woman's secret identity was discovered.

The amazed assembly joined together to glorify God and gave thanks to the Lord for filling Pelagia with His divine power and securing her incredible triumph over evil. Astonished by this accomplishment, the people spread the word of her marvelous feats, and crowds of people jammed the site, vying for the opportunity to pay their last respects. In the end, Pelagia — an ex-prostitute from Antioch and the muddy dove of Bishop Nonnos's dream — received an honorable burial in the Holy Land, with priests and candles and incense, close to the tomb of her heavenly Savior.

For her fast-acting ardor and irreversible repentance, we can choose to recall Pelagia's bold witness when we feel pulled back toward the thorny trap of sexual sin. "It is for freedom that Christ has set us free," the apostle Paul admonished. "Stand firm, then, and do not let yourselves be burdened again by a yoke of slavery" (Gal. 5:1). With our eyes wide open and our hearts set free, God will enable us to refuse all invitations to reenter that lamentable prison as we reach out to embrace Jesus, the one grand passion of our lives.

Open, Lord, my inward ear,
And bid my heart rejoice!
Bid my quiet spirit hear
Thy comfortable voice.
Never in the whirlwind found,
Or where earthquakes rock the place;
Still and silent is the sound,
The whisper of Thy grace.
From the world of sin, and noise,
And hurry, I withdraw;
For the small and inward voice
I wait, with humble awe.
Silent am I now, and still,
Dare not in Thy presence move;
To my waiting soul reveal
The secret of Thy love.
Lord, my time is in Thine hand,
My soul to Thee convert;
Thou canst make me understand,
Though I am slow of heart;
Thine, in whom I love and move,
Thine the work, the praise is Thine,
Thou art wisdom, power and love —
And all Thou art is mine.

—Charles Wesley (1707–1788)

CONCLUSION

*U*nlike Pelagia, Christians in the Western world do not rou-
tinely practice severe austerities in remote solitude away
from the sights and sounds of modern life. We remain attached to
the world, to a greater or lesser degree, and are frequently chal-
lenged by everyday trials and temptations within the context of
our complex, contemporary culture.

Needless to say, this can be really tough. Faced with the daily
demands of work, family, ministry, and friendships — not to men-
tion beauty expectations, financial pressures, health concerns, and
entertainment options — "dropping out," as Pelagia did, may seem
to be an appealing choice. In some ways, is it not more difficult to
be tried and tested on an ongoing basis, in the midst of demanding
human relationships, rather than to simply vanish?

It is here, within the multitextured design of life's continually
changing patterns, that we need to depend on God more than
ever.

Following Jesus in the midst of life as it actually is requires
the regular exercise of faith and a continuing commitment to pick
the right path. Yielding to God's grace and the Holy Spirit's direction is a strenuous process. But unlike a personal cardiovascular
fitness program, our walk with Christ is not one hundred percent
under our control.

We do not set the speed of our spiritual development. We cannot always avoid making mistakes. We will slip up along the
course God marks out for us. In spite of our best intentions. On a
regular basis.

Regardless of what we have done in the past, no matter when
the transgression took place — whether it was twenty years ago or
just this afternoon — we are called to discard our pride, admit our
sin, seek God's forgiveness, receive His pardon, and continue
walking. We cannot do this by ourselves, and should not be surprised to find that we need to continuously count on Jesus to supply us with the help and strength required. If we expect to do this
perfectly, propelled forward by our own muscle power, is that not
a certain setup for failure? You bet it is.

Says Dick Keyes, director of L'Abri Fellowship in the United States, "If your self-acceptance rests on maintaining an image of yourself as a nice, good person who never did anything wrong on purpose, then you cannot afford to allow much truth into your field of vision. True self-acceptance is in stark contrast to this self-delusion. Self-acceptance does not survive honesty; it rests on it."[10]

He reminds us: "If you are a Christian, your final environment is a world whose Creator forgives, accepts, and loves you in all your uniqueness. God not only loves you in this way, but He wants you to be always aware of it. He wants you to have that confidence and to live in it"[11].

Is this not incredible? We are not "women with a past" or "stupid women" for making the mistakes we regret — we are women with a hope and a future (Jer. 29:11), called according to God's purpose (Rom. 8:28), given an inheritance that can never perish, spoil, or fade (1 Peter 1:4). We have been chosen to receive a fresh start by faith in God, as Rahab was; giving us a new birth, as he provided for Pelagia, the Lord has called us "out of darkness into his wonderful light" (1 Peter 2:9). And still, God does not expect us to be perfect!

Do we really believe this? If we do, we will never be the same. It is truly humbling and liberating to know God loves us so much that, "If we confess our sins, he is faithful and just and will forgive us our sins and purify us from all unrighteousness" (1 John 1:9). Like Laurie, Carol, and Tricia, we, too, can believe that God saves us according to His promise.

It is not always easy to keep forgetting what lies behind us — the sins God has forgiven us for. Effort and endurance are required to turn away from painful memories that tie us to past events, threatening to pull us in the opposite direction from what lies ahead. Paul tells us to strain toward what we are called toward (Phil. 3:13–14). Moving on, in other words, is not an automatic process but a conscious, continuous choice.

Women who have walked away wounded from the "freedom" of sexual sin are finding themselves set free by Christ's love. And this is only one form of self-destructive behavior from which Jesus specializes in setting captives free.

If there is a particular area of your life that is difficult to deal with right now or you are facing a persistent problem that does not seem to go away, no matter how hard you try to get rid of it, pray for the grace of belief. Emotional wounds, especially deep ones, take time to heal. Be patient as God tends the wounds of your past. Trust Him to complete His perfect work in your life. Keep pressing on. And do not think it is strange when the Lord reminds you of what you need to work on along the way.

Points for Reflection

1. Believing that God loves and accepts me helps me to . . .
2. It is hard for me to believe that God forgives me when . . .
3. Rahab's protection during Jericho's downfall proves . . .
4. Like other women, I seek to be accepted by others and sometimes fear rejection for my Christian beliefs. This is especially
   true if . . .
5. The part of Pelagia's story that most impressed me is . . .
6. Right now, the most difficult part of turning away from my
   past is . . .

Prayer: God and Father, I am humbled by the grace of belief; by
faith in Christ, I affirm Your salvation working within me, healing the wounds of my past. Enlarge my capacity to believe, dear
Jesus. Amen.

⤙ 🍇 ⤚

I sought the LORD, and he answered me;
he delivered me from all my fears.
Those who look to him are radiant;
their faces are never covered with shame.
This poor man called, and the LORD heard him;
he saved him out of all his troubles.
The angel of the LORD encamps around
  those who fear him,
and he delivers them.
Taste and see that the Lord is good;
blessed is the man who takes refuge in him.
Fear the LORD, you his saints,
for those who fear him lack nothing.

—Psalm 34:4–9

I am not what I ought to be;
I am not what I would like to be;
I am not what I hope to be.
But I am not what I once was,
and by the grace of God, I am what I am.[12]

— John Newton (1725–1807)

Chapter Three

Surrender

~: ❦ :~

Cast yourself into the arms of God and be very sure
that if He wants anything of you, He will fit you for
the work and give you strength.[1]

— Philip Neri (1515–1595)

*L*ove has strong arms. Strong enough to steady my step if I
slip, to take hold of my shivering heart and restore its steady
rhythm. Love's arms lift me up and set me high upon a rock."[2] Jill
Briscoe's words confirm it: Whatever this day brings — a nagging
backache, a missed appointment, a phone that never quits — God's
strength will be sufficient. But the walk of faith requires ongoing
surrender to the Lord's loving care.

The grace of surrender helps us to give up the battle when we
still feel like fighting, if that is what God requires. It prompts us
to lay down our time and talents before Christ's throne when our
preference is to "make things happen." Surrender leads us to say,
like Charles de Foucald a century ago, "My Father, I abandon
myself to You. Do with me as You will. Whatever You may do
with me, I thank You. I am prepared for anything, I accept everything, provided Your will is fulfilled in me and in all creatures —
I ask for nothing more, my God. I place my soul in Your hands. I
give it to You, my God, with all the love of my heart, because I
love You."[3] Through surrender, we find grace in the midst of
struggle, peace in the aftermath of pain, strength in a place of
powerlessness.

Sounds nice, does it not — to just go with the flow, offering no
resistance to the changing tides of reality, with a tranquil "live and
let live" outlook? But that is not surrender — it is compliance.

Surrender means giving up, as opposed to giving in. Through surrender, there comes a genuine relinquishing of our rights to Jesus Christ as the Lord of our lives.

My friend Sarah, in the hospital this week for cancer treatment, expresses her recent encounter with the grace of surrender this way: "Lately, I've felt as though I'm on a raft floating down a river. One minute, everything's quiet and peaceful as my small boat reaches the smooth surface of an eddy, a brief break in the tumult. Then, without warning, it hits. Drifting slowly downstream, the pace picks up, I go round the next bend and slam full force into white-water rapids."

Choosing her words carefully, she explains, "I can't predict what's going to happen next. I don't even know if I'll make it. And I really dislike not being in control. But God has helped me to understand that my ability to direct the course of my life is an illusion. I never was in control, even though it seemed that way to me."

After a short pause, Sarah struggled to clarify her feelings. "Yesterday, I got pretty angry with God about the whole leukemia deal. I figured, He can take it — He already knows what's going on inside my heart anyway. I felt a lot more peaceful afterward, because I was totally honest with Him about how I felt."

I could tell that this was not an easy thing for my typically cool, calm, collected, and ever-competent friend to admit.

"This morning, I woke up, thanked God for another new day, and then I realized: No matter what happens, I win," announced Sarah decisively. "Whether the leukemia goes into remission or I go to be with the Lord — whichever He decides is best for me — either way, I will come out of this thing a winner."

Although she faces ongoing uncertainty about her physical health and realizes additional high-risk treatments lie ahead, Sarah's openhearted surrender to the Lord in her time of crisis has touched many friends, family members, medical workers, and professional colleagues in extraordinary ways. With honesty and grace, she is learning to trust God with her future, whatever it turns out to be.

I am also reminded of another woman when I think of the unique quality of Christian surrender — the life-changing experience of a twenty-one-year-old expectant mother named Joanna. Puzzled by an unrelenting pain in her abdomen, the first-time mom did not know what to think about her discomfort. It did not feel like labor, but how would she know what labor was supposed to feel like if she had never encountered it before?

While waiting to be examined in a labor room at an Atlanta hospital, Joanna's electronic monitor strip showed no significant uterine contractions and a regular fetal heart rate. A check for cervical dilation soon showed that active labor had not started.

The nurse-midwife recommended an ultrasound scan. Given her client's continuing complaints of sharp abdominal pain, the birth attendant suggested the diagnostic procedure to clarify the placenta's location and condition. As Matthew, Joanna's husband, walked beside the wheelchair down the hallway to the ultrasound room, he seemed somewhat curious but not very concerned about the painless procedure. He had not seen the sonogram performed earlier in the pregnancy, and wanted to be there when this one was done.

Assisting his sedated wife onto the vinyl-padded exam table, he noted the time and asked the technician a few questions; Joanna smiled as the cold gel spurted out of its plastic container onto her tightly stretched skin. Holding her hand, Matthew gazed at the monitor as the technician rhythmically swept the diagnostic wand back and forth over his wife's abdomen. The images on the screen were splotchy and difficult for Matthew to decipher. He did not notice that the technician was scanning the same areas again and again, typing in the words *ventricle, bladder,* and *lumbar spine* as she paused periodically to punch in detailed commands. To the inexperienced couple, the gray shadows and shifting patterns on the black-and-white screen revealed only a busy little person bouncing around inside Joanna's fluid-filled womb.

Standing silently nearby, I had observed almost everything — the technician's cautious concern, the radiologist's careful concentration, the stark sonogram display. As a veteran childbirth educator and birthing assistant, I was fairly certain of what the news would be but could only watch with increasing concern as the two anxious parents I had volunteered to accompany through labor returned quietly to their hospital room.

Deciding that it would be better to let the midwife present the test results at the appropriate time, I followed my dozing daughter and exhausted son-in-law back to the maternity wing and sat in a rocking chair while we waited for the midwife's official report.

Watching Joanna rest peacefully, I prayed for the safe delivery of my first grandchild and thought about the possible impact of the diagnosis on my children's lives. I asked God to supply my daughter, my firstborn, with special strength. Whenever tears welled up in my eyes, I pretended that I needed to use the rest room and dabbed furtively at my mascara-covered lashes with cold water. I told myself that I could wait to express the emotions surging up within me at a later time. For now, my daughter needed encouragement, not a maternal sobbing explosion.

Two hours later, the midwife's explanation did not surprise me. "The ultrasound showed that the placenta is fine, but we have some concerns about the baby," said Joanna's birth attendant somberly. "Did you have any tests done during your pregnancy to check for neural tube defects?"

"No. The only ultrasound I had was on a small machine at the office. When the midwife couldn't find the fetal heartbeat a few months ago, she used it to locate the baby's position," my daughter answered.

"Well, what today's sonogram showed us is that your baby has a neural tube defect. It's called hydrocephalus, or fluid on the brain. And, from the size of the baby's bladder, it looks like the baby isn't urinating properly, so there may be significant impairment of nerve function. This may be a result of a condition known as spina bifida, which involves a failure of the bones of the spine to close around the baby's spinal cord in the early weeks of prenatal development — though we didn't see clear evidence of any lesions along the baby's backbone."

There it was. In one long, uninterrupted, solemnly spoken statement, the midwife declared it, as if she knew from experience that taking any long pauses to give the strange-sounding infor-

mation time to sink in would make the announcement too difficult. For once, I did not envy the midwife for her job.

My daughter and son-in-law reacted with a kind of calm
courage to the succinct summary. Thankfully, their love for their
little one proved much stronger than their fear. The diagnosis did
not detract from their bond with their baby, although it would be
tempting at such a time to succumb to a scientifically induced, self-
protective shift in attachment toward a preborn child. I was proud
of my kids. Quite simply, they refused to allow the sonogram's
graphic power to destroy their glad anticipation.

Understandably, there were tears when Abigail arrived safely
into Joanna's arms at last, only to be whisked away immediately
to the neonatal intensive care unit to await her first surgery. But
more important, there was joy.

In the past year and a half, I have seen my daughter changed
by motherhood and affliction, and marvel at her growing willingness to listen from her appointed place in God's waiting room,
wondering what new test of faith tomorrow may bring, exploring
new dimensions of trust in her Savior, postponing professional
plans. However reluctant her affirmation of God's direction for
her life may be at times, I know that Joanna has often taken her
stubborn heart and laid it as a sacrifice before the Savior's throne.
Like most of us, she is still struggling, still hurting, still searching. But in an era when many say no to the Lord, she has repeatedly answered yes.

In my friend Sarah's and my daughter Joanna's lives, I have
witnessed the reality of God's grace of surrender supplied at crit-
ical moments. The depth of peace they have experienced when
others would wilt defies explanation — its unexpected appearance
has surprised and amazed us all, a gift they say they did not
deserve and cannot explain, a calming force that arrived when
they least expected it, supplying them with enough strength to
keep going under the heavy weight of ongoing therapies and
unknown prognoses.

Although the circumstances in Sarah's and Joanna's lives are
very different from those that Jesus' mother faced, I sometimes
think of Mary when I consider their willingness to give themselves

to God, to depend on His strength instead of their own — not giving in, but giving up — reaching for the faith to believe their heavenly Father can be trusted to preserve and protect His family. "In His will is our peace," Dante Alligheri observed. Yet, this is a mystery, is it not? For a woman to find joy in the midst of her greatest anguish — how can it be? In the following familiar story, Mary's surrender to God's will makes this paradox more clear to us.

Mary's Story

We can easily picture her face and form. Whether smiling sweetly from the surface of a painted canvas or captured in an ethereal pose carved in pale-colored marble, the Madonna portraits of Rembrandt, Caravaggio, and other renowned artists are the images of Mary we remember. Thus, it is the mature, benevolent, loving mother we call to mind — the woman Mary became long after God's messenger first appeared on her doorstep — not a shivering adolescent struck by holy glory.

· Barely beyond childhood, betrothed to a descendant of David, bound by centuries of Jewish tradition, Mary was forever set apart from all other women as Gabriel proclaimed: "Greetings, most favored one! The Lord is with you" (Luke 1:28 NEB).

Greatly troubled, the girl immediately took stock of the situation and wondered what the heavenly stranger's "Greetings" might mean: *Am I going to die? Why is the angel using the title most favored one? What is happening to me? Where's Mother? What in heaven and on earth is going on?* Whatever her thoughts may have been, however, Mary apparently did not cry out for help, or turn and run.

Perhaps noticing Mary's trembling, the angel's next words seem intentionally soothing. "Do not be afraid, Mary, you have found favor with God," he reassured her (Luke 1:30). And then, Gabriel issued the world's most amazing announcement: "You will be with child and give birth to a son, and you are to give him the name Jesus. He will be great and will be called the Son of the Most High. The Lord God will give him the throne of his father David, and he will reign over the house of Jacob forever; his kingdom will never end" (Luke 1:31–33).

Through our knowledge of the Bible, attendance at repeated Christmas pageants, memorization of "Silent Night," and viewing of television dramatizations, we already know what the angel told

Mary. It is old news to us, a fact of history long accepted by Christian believers. As a result, it is nearly impossible for us to imagine what it must have really been like for the young teen girl when these words were spoken for the first time.

Stunned by the infinite implications of the angel's words, Mary simply asked: "How?"

Encountering Divinity

We live by faith, not by sight. 2 Corinthians 5:7

As a betrothed young woman soon to be married, Mary must have been well-versed in female physiology — enough to understand that the matter of pregnancy, at least for her, was out of the question.

Strict codes of conduct governed Jewish sexual standards and women's hygiene practices in her small Galilean village of Nazareth. Her future husband would legally divorce her if she was found to be carrying another man's child. Mary was a devout virgin. What went through her mind when she was told she would be pregnant before her wedding? And who would have believed the truth had she confirmed it?

Shattered plans, revoked vows, and a canceled ceremony loomed ahead. Faced with history's grand turning point in an exclusive preview of things to come, Mary reasonably wanted to know, *How?*

Is this not a refreshing response? Would not a girl of about fourteen years of age, told by a gleaming heavenly being that she is about to experience an unplanned pregnancy, naturally want to know more about what was going on?

The entire scene, as written by Luke, portrays Mary as a wonderfully real, bright young woman with her head planted squarely on her shoulders, not in the clouds — someone you and I would find easy to talk to — a brave, faith-filled Jewish mother-to-be ready to raise God's Son with humor and candor and grace. The Mary depicted in this portrait is more earthy and far less delicate than the idealized mother we see on display at the National Gallery of Art. Can you picture one of these smooth-skinned women with the peaches-and-cream complexions fainting, right on the spot, if presented with such startlingly explicit news? But when the angel's announcement arrives, the real Mary — the Mary we see in the Bible, not in the Louvre — fearlessly wondered, *How?*

And so the angel explained it: "The Holy Spirit will come upon you, and the power of the Most High will overshadow you. So the holy one to be born will be called the Son of God. Even Elizabeth your relative is going to have a child in her old age, and she who was said to be barren is in her sixth month. For nothing is impossible with God" (Luke 1:35–37).

While many take years to prepare and launch their ministries, Mary was granted no time. When others count costs and weigh risks, Mary could not do a careful cost-benefit analysis. Where some choose to go only after the destination is made perfectly clear, Mary had no idea how far her journey would take her. She believed, and she surrendered, and that was all. "I am the Lord's servant," was Mary's answer. "May it be to me as you have said" (Luke 1:38).

Then Gabriel was gone.

Womanly Wisdom

> *Praise be to the God and Father of our Lord Jesus Christ, the Father of compassion and the God of all comfort.* 2 Corinthians 1:3

*T*ry to imagine what it must have been like for Mary the day after the angel's alarming appearance, waking up the next morning, with a full night's sleep separating her from the radiant visitor's prophecy, in those first few moments as she started to feel conscious of birds chirping outside, sunshine beaming through the window, the sound of a rickety wooden cart rolling by, the soothing awareness of her bed underneath her body.

For just a minute or so, everything felt routine, normal, familiar. Then, the angel's words echoed in Mary's mind. She opened her eyes and saw the place where the angel had stood.

As the realization of what happened the day before flooded Mary's entire being, we may assume her heartbeat quickened, her breathing rate increased, and her throat went dry. It is easy to think that Mary placed her hand gently on her abdomen and pondered, *Is the Son of God growing within me now?* Lying quietly in the early morning sunlight, looking back from the perspective of a bright new day, how utterly strange and marvelous it must have been. Jesus was on His way!

In a culture where preconception planning, home pregnancy tests, early prenatal visits, and best-selling mother-care manuals are widely available, signs of conception may be readily recognized. Mary's pregnancy, however, was confirmed in a delightfully different way.

Quickly preparing to leave for her relative Elizabeth's house, Mary wasted no time. She needed to be where God wanted her to go. There would be no lies given to her family — or Joseph — so she had to leave. Setting off for a town in the hill country of Judea, Mary was alone with God in her thoughts along the way. The angel said that Elizabeth was going to have a child! What an emotion-packed journey that must have been for the young expectant mother, carrying her precious secrets as she slowly grew accustomed to the impossible truth of the Messiah's unique form of arrival.

Stepping inside the home of Zechariah, Mary's greeting must have come as something of a surprise to her elder kinswoman. Upon hearing Mary's words, Elizabeth's baby jumped inside her womb. Immediately filled with the Holy Spirit, she loudly exclaimed: "Blessed are you among women, and blessed is the child you will bear! But why am I so favored, that the mother of my Lord should come to me? As soon as the sound of your greeting reached my ears, the baby in my womb leaped for joy. Blessed is she who has believed that what the Lord has said to her will be accomplished!" (Luke 1:42–45).

In this wonderful way, the awesome news of Jesus' conception was confirmed. With an outburst of praise and worship inspired by the Holy Spirit, Mary joyously lifted her voice to the skies and rejoiced with all of her strength.

Forty Weeks' Waiting

. . . who comforts us in all our troubles, so that we can
comfort those in any trouble with the comfort we ourselves
have received from God. 2 Corinthians 1:4

For about three months, Mary stayed with Elizabeth — enough time for her pregnancy to become established and for the purposes of God to continue to unfold. What was it like for Mary during these early weeks, as she sensed Jesus' presence for the first time?

Unquestionably, Mary began to encounter some of the usual physical changes that all expectant women experience: weight gain; increased breathing, heart, and metabolic rates; fatigue; digestive and postural changes; and more. Did she feel sickened by kitchen smells? Was she more tired than usual? Were there foods she craved? Probably so.

She also must have thought often about her beloved Joseph, and prayed for her family back home, wondering when her wedding would take place. Throughout that first trimester, Elizabeth's loving presence and kind advice must have been a healing balm for the young mother-to-be.

After Mary's return to Nazareth, Joseph was forced to face his future bride's pregnancy for the first time. In those days, a betrothed Jewish couple were called "husband and wife," joined by a binding relationship that could only be severed through divorce. Wishing to avoid Mary's certain exposure to public accusation and disgrace, Joseph, an honorable and righteous man, decided to proceed discreetly in this direction. But an angel of the Lord appeared to him in a dream, and told Joseph not to be afraid to take Mary home to be his wife. A brief description of Jesus' conception convinced the stunned sleeper to remain true to his vows.

From that day forward, Joseph and Mary lived together chastely as a betrothed couple. Here again, as in so many other places in the Bible, we see God's perfect will enacted in the midst of tremendous personal upheaval and drastically altered plans, for Joseph and Mary's marriage was delayed until after Jesus' birth!

(Luke 2:5). To make matters even more complicated, the Emperor Caesar Augustus issued a decree for a census to be taken of the entire Roman world that required everyone to return to his or her town of origin to register.

So, in the final weeks of her pregnancy, Mary packed up a few necessities and, leaving the familiarity of her home and family behind, began her arduous journey through the hills with Joseph, along rough desert roads on the way to Bethlehem.

Clinging to the Promise

And God is able to make all grace abound to you, so that in all things at all times, having all that you need, you will abound in every good work. 2 Corinthians 9:8

The scene of the holy family, with Joseph slowly leading the way on foot and Mary riding on the back of a donkey behind him, is one we are well-acquainted with. But what was this episode of the Christmas saga actually like for Mary? Nine months pregnant, sitting for what must have seemed like endless hours on a dusty, blanket-covered donkey's back, unprotected from the desert sun and arid heat — did the discomfort make her weep?

In the last months of pregnancy, a substance called relaxin causes the expectant mother's joints to soften and shift, creating changes in her bones' alignment. A helpful hormone, it eases birth by allowing for a slight expansion of the baby's passageway. But it also makes sitting in one place for very long unusually uncomfortable.

With the "dropping" of the baby into the pelvis, which typically occurs in a first pregnancy at least four weeks prior to the onset of labor, Mary's abdominal muscles stretched, exaggerating the curve of her lower back, making it more vulnerable to strain and pain. And as a result of the downward movement of her baby's position, the pressure of the baby's head on internal organs created greater sensitivity to sudden motion, making frequent relief stops unavoidable. She was also warmer and more tired than usual: A pregnant woman's metabolism is much busier than an average person's, making her feel flushed when others complain that the temperature is too cool. It is also common to experience stiffness and swelling, or edema, of the ankles, feet, face, and hands on hot days. While traveling to Bethlehem through the hills, it is likely that Mary felt most, if not all, of these things.

As the womb prepares for its future work, periodic muscle contractions mandated by the mother's reproductive system recur regularly — an involuntary fitness routine designed to strengthen the uterus for childbirth. To prevent labor from starting too early, a special hormone, progesterone, relaxes smooth muscle tissues throughout the mother's body, slowing down digestion. Consequently, a meal eaten at six o'clock in the evening tends to remain capable of producing a sensation of fullness at bedtime. Sleep is further disrupted by frequent urination and difficulty finding a position that is conducive to sound rest. Dreams become more vivid. Movements of the baby, while at times endearing, are nevertheless irksome if a tiny foot suddenly jabs mom's ribs. In a very real sense, the mother is eating — and digesting, excreting, breathing, metabolizing, and resting — for herself and her baby.

On the long journey to Bethlehem, Mary must have longed to hold Jesus in her arms and lie peacefully with her newborn, to rest without the relentless weight bearing down on her weary back and body.

The Surrender of Birth

This service that you perform is not only supplying the needs of God's people but is also overflowing in many expressions of thanks to God. 2 Corinthians 9:12

*I*n the days just preceding a woman's entry into active labor, a hormonal phenomenon widely known as "the burst of energy" spurs an expectant mother to do all sorts of things she normally would not have the stamina or enthusiasm to accomplish. It is not unheard of, for example, for the soon-to-be mother to bake six dozen cookies, clean the refrigerator, wax floors, and do several loads of laundry — all in one afternoon.

Mary had no house to focus her nesting instinct upon, no permanent place to stay, no home hearth to cook on. Dirt roads and dry hills, the changing scenery of an unplanned-for existence, comprised her daily landscape. There was no nursery to decorate, no midwife to talk to, no female friends to fellowship with, no nurturing mother nearby.

Upon reaching Bethlehem, Mary must have keenly felt the absence of her family. The city was overcrowded, bursting at the seams, as people gathered for the census and filled every rented room in town. More than likely, Mary was showing signs of impending labor as Joseph searched in vain for some small corner where the couple could comfortably rest. Her contractions were probably growing more frequent as Joseph looked for a place to settle for the night. At some point, Mary's husband knew that they could not wait any longer.

Was it in a moment of Spirit-led inspiration that Joseph, realizing that the baby was coming, saw the stable and took his laboring wife to lie down in the hay by a manger?

Giving birth is hard work, they found. As the muscles press the baby down through the mother's body, tissues stretch open to make room for the little one's passage. A woman becomes completely absorbed in this process, unable to do anything but concentrate on coping with each contraction, one at a time, and finally, to push with her entire being as the baby leaves her womb.

There is little in our world to adequately prepare one's heart and mind for childbearing. While the body performs its work, a woman engages in an act of concentrated effort unlike any other natural physical phenomenon as she lets go of the child growing within her and brings forth new life.

When the appointed time arrived, God gave Mary the strength to accomplish the work He had uniquely called her to do: to bring forth the Savior of the world, a baby boy named Jesus, in an obscure stable somewhere in Bethlehem, far away from home. At the end of a long and unexpected journey, Mary surrendered herself to her labor, and was thankful.

Vibia Perpetua's Story

~ 🍇 ~

or Vibia Perpetua, an early Christian martyr, the risk of surrender required the highest sacrifice.

Born around 181 A.D., Perpetua was the well-educated daughter of a wealthy nobleman living in the Roman-occupied city of
Carthage, the populous North African commerce center. Christianity was still in its initial stages of germination. Numerous
vibrant churches, planted by Roman converts, were sprouting up
across the area, and while most believers' social and economic
backgrounds were deeply rooted in the lower or middle classes,
the Gospel had yet to be successfully sown among the most influential citizens of Carthage.

A young woman in her early twenties and the mother of an
infant son, Perpetua was widely known for her beauty and intelligence. One of the first women of her social rank in the city to
become a Christian, her faith was marked by a generous willingness to give up material comforts in favor of sacrificial abandon-
ment to God right from the start. Perpetua's decision to follow the
Lord probably shocked her leisure-loving peers; perhaps it even
provoked her husband to desert her, for he is never mentioned in
the historical accounts of her life: a journal written by Perpetua
herself; the firsthand narration of one of her companions, Saturnus; and an eyewitness's record.

Under an edict banning fresh conversions to Christianity
issued by the Roman emperor Septimus Severus, the young
believer's decision to follow the Lord was a mortally dangerous
commitment. In light of Severus's decree, Perpetua's choice was
this: to denounce Christ and remain alive, or remain true to her
King and be put to death. Though she was a recent convert, the
courageous woman never wavered in the certainty of her selection.

One of the first persons to be arrested, imprisoned, and sentenced under the emperor's new mandate, Perpetua, with the other members of her prayer group — the deacon Saturnus, her teacher; Felicitas, her pregnant slave; Felicitas' husband, Revocatus; and two Christian brothers, Secundulus and Saturninus — was quickly condemned to suffer martyrdom. She was sentenced with her five friends to face wild animals, then execution by a gladiator's sword, in the arena.

Daughter, Mother, and Sister

*But we have this treasure in jars of clay
to show that this all-surpassing power is from
God and not from us.* 2 Corinthians 4:7

Though Perpetua's courageous choice was luminously clear to her, it was nonetheless clouded by family ties. Although she and her companions were confident that their martyrdom would win many people to Christ, Perpetua struggled with her elderly, resistant father, who did everything possible to save his daughter from dying a terrible death.

But Perpetua would not be moved. When the exasperated patriarch finally flew into a rage, saying that he would beat Perpetua into submission if it would save her life, his desperate threats were repeatedly stonewalled by his daughter's serene assurances. Nothing, she assured him, could convince her to turn away from God's calling upon her life. "Father," she said calmly during one of these disputes, "do you see this vessel lying here? Can one call anything by any other name than what it is? So neither can I call myself anything else than what I am — a Christian."[4]

The day after this particular confrontation, Perpetua and her companions were seized by the authorities and thrown in prison. Openly confessing in her journal that she was "very much afraid" upon her arrival there, it is unlikely that Perpetua had ever experienced such blatant cruelty before. Packed crowds, profane soldiers, diseased convicts, cramped quarters, and soaring temperatures, combined with Perpetua's obvious maternal concerns about her infant son, must have mounted a dizzily disorienting attack on the refined woman's cultivated sensibilities and resolute strength. Surely it was a direct answer to prayer when two church deacons successfully arranged to have Perpetua and Felicitas transferred to a more agreeable area of the jail. Here, Perpetua became reconciled to her circumstances, observing in her journal:

> I nursed my child, who was already weak from hunger. In my anxiety for the infant I spoke to my mother about him, tried to console my brother, and asked that they care for my son. I suffered intensely because I sensed their agony on my account. These were the trials I had to endure for many days. Then I was granted the privilege of having my son remain with me in prison. Being relieved of my anxiety and concern for the infant, I immediately regained my strength. Suddenly the prison became my palace, and I loved being there rather than any other place.[5]

Before the Tribunal

> *For just as the sufferings of Christ flow over into our lives, so also through Christ our comfort overflows.* 2 Corinthians 1:5

ut of suffering have emerged the strongest souls; the most massive characters are seamed with scars; martyrs have put on their coronation robes glittering with fire, and through their tears have the sorrowful first seen the gates of heaven,"[6] wrote Edward Hubbell Chapin in the nineteenth century — a fitting description of Perpetua, who was strengthened daily by God's grace and encouraged by the Holy Spirit's enlivening presence as her faith grew rapidly after being reunited with her son. But on the day before she received her summons to appear before the Roman tribunal, Perpetua faced her father in yet another attempt to divert her deadly course of action.

"Daughter, have pity on my gray head," he pleaded. "Have pity on your father if I have the honor to be called father by you, if with these hands I have brought you to the prime of your life, and if I have always favored you above your brothers, do not abandon me to the reproach of men.

"Consider your brothers; consider your mother and your aunt; consider your son who cannot live without you," her father implored. "Give up your stubbornness before you destroy all of us."

"These were things my father said out of love, kissing my hands and throwing himself at my feet," she recorded after the visit. "With tears he called me not daughter, but woman. I was very upset because of my father's condition. He was the only member of my family who would find no reason for joy in my suffering." Attempting to assuage her father's grief, Perpetua told him: "This will be done on that scaffold which God has willed; for know that we have been placed not in our own power but God's."[7]

The following day, Hilarian, the Procurator of Carthage, asked Perpetua, "Art thou a Christian?"

"I am," she answered plainly. "I cannot forsake my faith for freedom."[8]

Perpetua's father, who was listening in the audience, ran to rescue his daughter when he heard these words, well aware that her conviction would inevitably lead to death in the arena. Hilarian ordered the man to be beaten with a rod. As Perpetua watched the pitiful sight, she wrote later that it was as if she herself had received the battering.

Perpetua's diary shows that she felt deeply saddened by the patriarch's coming bereavement during her father's last visit before the Games. Still, he was unsuccessful in his final attempt to dissuade his daughter as he spoke to her for the last time.

Answered Prayers

> *So we fix our eyes not on what is seen, but on what is unseen. For what is seen is temporary, but what is unseen is eternal.* 2 Corinthians 4:18

aptized only a short time before her arrest, Perpetua was evidently prepared in advance to meet her martyrdom. Rising from her baptismal waters, she remarked, "The Holy Spirit has inspired me to pray for nothing but patience under bodily pains."[9]

As she waited for her execution day, Perpetua experienced a variety of visions while in prison. Before the trial, she prayed fervently that God would reveal the tribunal's decision. In a dream, she saw a golden ladder, with "every kind of iron instrument, swords, lances, hooks, [and] daggers" on its sides, reaching up into heaven. Under the ladder was a monstrous dragon frightening the climbers. Perpetua saw her teacher, Saturnus, climb up first; then he turned and called for her to follow, cautioning his pupil to be wary lest the dragon bite her. She replied, "In the name of Jesus Christ, he shall not hurt me," and, as she ascended the ladder, the dragon cowered beneath her feet.[10]

Perpetua dreamed also of seeing a large garden where an aged shepherd sat, milking ewes. Surrounded by a throng of people dressed in white, he offered cheese to the young woman and her companions, and as they ate it, the assembly cried, "Amen," waking Perpetua with their sweet-sounding voices. When she discussed the dream with her companions in prison, they interpreted it as the Lord's telling them they would be martyred soon, and they prayed to God to make them worthy of their calling.

On a different occasion, Perpetua had a vision of being led into the arena, where she was stripped of her clothing and became a man. In a masculine form, she engaged in unarmed, single combat with the Devil in the figure of an Egyptian, whom Perpetua vanquished and declared victory over as she stood on the defeated Enemy's head.

Another answer to prayer came when Felicitas, Perpetua's maidservant, gave birth one month before her expected due date. Because it was forbidden to execute a pregnant woman, Felicitas became increasingly concerned that she would not be martyred with her friends and asked God to grant her an early delivery. Felicitas's labor contractions began while the group prayed for her.

As she worked to bring forth her child, the prison's midwife mockingly remarked, "If you cry out now, what will you do when you are thrown to beasts in the arena?" Perpetua shares Felicitas's reply in her journal: "I myself suffer not, but then another shall be in me who shall suffer for me, because I am to suffer for him."[11]

A baby girl, who was later adopted and raised by Felicitas' sister, arrived just three days before the women walked into the arena.

Coronation Day

Because of the service by which you have proved yourselves,
men will praise God for the obedience that accompanies your
confession of the gospel of Christ. 2 Corinthians 9:13

For their last meal, Perpetua and her friends declined to partake in the sumptuous banquet customarily provided on the eve of the Games and enjoyed an agape meal together — a sacred symbol of love and kindness frequently celebrated by the early Christians.

On March 7, 203 A.D., the day of their execution, the six saints departed from the prison "joyfully as though they were on their way to heaven." An assortment of animals had been specially prepared for killing them: bears, leopards, and a wild boar for the men, and a crazed heifer for the women. Perpetua refused to wear the dress of Ceres, the Roman goddess of agriculture, and sang a psalm of praise as she entered the arena with the others.

"If there was any trembling, it was from joy, not fear," reported an observer, who also wrote:

> After being stripped and enmeshed in nets, the women were led into the arena. How horrified the people were as they saw that one was a young girl and the other, her breasts dripping with milk, had just recently given birth to a child. Consequently both were recalled and dressed in loosely fitting gowns. Perpetua was tossed first and fell on her back. She sat up, and being more concerned with her sense of modesty than with her pain, covered her thighs with her gown, which had been torn down one side. Then finding her hair-clip that had fallen out, she pinned back her loose hair, thinking it not proper for a martyr to suffer with disheveled hair; it might seem that she was mourning in her hour of triumph. Then she stood up. Noticing that Felicitas was badly bruised, she went to her, reaching out her hands and helping her to her feet.[12]

Returning to the amphitheater's gate for a rest after the crowd had cried out, "Enough!" Perpetua asked incredulously, "When are we going to be thrown to that heifer or whatever it is?"[13]

Apparently unaware of the extent or severity of her injuries, the dying saint felt no pain.

The Kiss of Courage

But thanks be to God, who always leads us in triumphal procession in Christ and through us spreads everywhere the fragrance of the knowledge of him. 2 Corinthians 2:14

Refusing to believe that she had been harmed yet, Perpetua was shown the marks on her body and reminded of the tear in her tattered dress. Asking for her brother, she exhorted him to remain true to Christ and sent a message with him to take to her family, urging them to love one another without permitting "our suffering to keep them from the faith."

Saturninus, who had faced a wild boar unhurt but was subsequently mangled by a leopard, joined the other martyrs as the savage swarm of onlookers urged them onward:

And when the crowd demanded that the prisoners be brought out into the open so that they might feast their eyes on death by the sword, they voluntarily arose and moved where the crowd wanted them. Before doing so they kissed each other so that their martyrdom would be completely perfected by the rite of the kiss of peace. The others, without making a sound, were killed by the sword . . . but Perpetua, to feel some of the pain, groaning as she was struck between the ribs, took the gladiator's trembling hand and guided it to her throat. Perhaps it was that so great a woman, feared as she was by the unclean spirit, could not have been slain had she herself not willed it.[14]

Buried with her companions in Carthage at the Basilica Majorum, Perpetua's martyrdom soon became famous among Christians everywhere. And the church grew as the news of her heroic surrender was heard across the empire, just as they prayed it would.

~: 🍇 :~

Take my life, and let it be
Consecrated, Lord, to Thee.
Take my moments and my days;
Let them flow in ceaseless praise.
Take my hands, and let them move
At the impulse of Thy love.
Take my feet, and let them be
Swift and beautiful for Thee.
Take my voice, and let me sing
Always, only, for my King.
Take my lips, and let them be
Filled with messages for Thee.
Take my silver and my gold;
Not a mite would I withhold.
Take my intellect, and use
Every power as Thou choose.
Take my will, and make it Thine;
It shall be no longer mine.
Take my heart, it is Thine own;
It shall be Thy royal throne.
Take my love, I pour
At Thy feet its treasure-store.
Take myself, and I will be
Ever, only, all for Thee.

— Frances Ridley Havergal (1836–1879)

CONCLUSION

*C*ome to me. . . ." When the circumstances of life are beyond our ability to bear them, when there seems to be no way for things to work out, when rapids hit and the boat threatens to capsize at any moment, when a sudden change in life plans cancels our dreams and reroutes the future, Jesus stands before us, and with His arms opened wide, extends this incredible invitation. Surrendering our burdens at His feet and placing each heavy parcel before the cross, we can choose to close our ears to competing commands and confusing directions, and listen for God's voice alone.

Jesus said, "Come to me, all you who are weary and burdened, and I will give you rest. Take my yoke upon you and learn from me, for I am gentle and humble in heart, and you will find rest for your souls. For my yoke is easy and my burden is light" (Matt. 11:28–30). How could Mary have found her burden light on the way to Bethlehem, riding over bumpy roads on the back of a lumbering donkey? Was Perpetua's yoke easy when she faced her father's final, desperate pleas? Do Sarah and Joanna think that their present limitations are easy? These women's stories prompt us to remember that God's graces appear in the midst of a consecrated life as it is actually lived, not in some far-off realm set apart from real human emotional experience.

Surrender never discounts or denies the reality of our suffering. When Jesus agonizingly prayed in the Garden of Gethsemane, "Father, if you are willing, take this cup from me; yet not my will but yours be done" (Luke 22:42), there can be no doubt that He knew what was at stake in the battle looming ahead. Quietly facing his accusers, He submitted to their authority, fully recognizing the costs involved. He understood what the terms of His surrender would be.

But that is not all: By laying down His life before His enemies in obedience to God's will, Jesus demolished the opposition.

Through surrender — bowing before God's mighty throne, laying each struggle before our Father in heaven, casting out all grief and heartache, giving up to Jesus every source of suffering and sin — we participate, with Christ, in His kingdom's victories. We cannot do it on our own. We are not supposed to even try to do it on our own. Heeding the Lord's command to surrender, we are continually surprised to find that, somehow, in a way that is totally beyond our comprehension, *He triumphs through us.*

"With what magnificent confidence you may step out into the future when once you have consented to die to your own self-effort, and to make yourself available as a redeemed sinner to all that God has made available to you in His risen Son!"[15] proclaims Major Ian Thomas, the founder and director of Torchbearers International.

"To be in Christ — that is redemption; but for Christ to be in you — that is sanctification! To be in Christ — that makes you fit for heaven; but for Christ to be in you — that makes you fit for earth! To be in Christ — that changes our destination; but for Christ to be in you — that changes your destiny! The one makes heaven your home — the other makes this world His workshop."[16] Thus, Major Thomas exuberantly explains the dynamic existence available to all who surrender to Jesus Christ as their risen Savior — the Lord's sanctifying strength mysteriously perfected in human weakness.

Consider the description in God's Word of all believers in whom the indwelling power of Jesus Christ resides: "But all of us who are Christians have no veils on our faces, but reflect like mirrors the glory of the Lord. We are transformed in ever-increasing splendor into his own image and and this is the work of the Lord who is the Spirit." (2 Cor. 3:18 PHILLIPS). As women who are currently undergoing this breathtaking transformation, we place our hope in the same Lord who defended His beloved on Calvary. As incredible as it may seem to us now, one day we will wake up to find ourselves made over into a flawless masterpiece fit to spend eternity in God's glorious presence.

"Holiness in us is the copy or transcript of the holiness that is in Christ," believed Philip Henry. "As the wax hath line for line from the seal, and the child feature for feature from the Father, so is holiness in us from him."[17] Do you believe that the beauty of holiness is God's promised gift to "ordinary" people instead of something that only a few outstanding saints achieve?

Take heart, then. Pray for the grace of surrender. Receive all of the peace, and joy, and love that Jesus freely offers. He is waiting. His arms are open. What He has done for the greatest saints, He surely can do for you and me.

Points for Reflection

1. Surrender is best described as . . .
2. When I am weary and heavyhearted, Jesus comforts me by . . .
3. Mary's story reminds me of . . .
4. At this time in my life the most difficult area to surrender to Christ's lordship is . . .
5. As I read about Vibia Perpetua, I thought about . . .
6. Fixing my thoughts on the Lord's surrender on the cross encourages me to . . .

Prayer: *Lord, tune our ears to the timbre of Your voice. Teach us to trust that through You, triumph results from surrender. Help us to come running when You call; direct us to follow where You lead; strengthen us to do all that You ask. In Jesus Christ. Amen.*

As for God, his way is perfect;
the word of the LORD is flawless.
He is a shield
for all who take refuge in him.
For who is God besides the LORD?
And who is the Rock except our God?
It is God who arms me with strength
and makes my way perfect.
He makes my feet like the feet of a deer;
he enables me to stand on the heights.

—Psalm 18:30–33

∴ ❦ ∾

O to grace how great a debtor
Daily I'm constrained to be!
Let Thy goodness, like a fetter,
Bind my wandering heart to Thee:
Prone to wander, Lord, I feel it,
Prone to leave the God I love;
Here's my heart, O take and seal it;
Seal it for Thy courts above.

— Robert Robinson (1735–1790)

Chapter Four

Obedience

God insists that He set up His throne in the heart,
and reign in it, without a rival. If we keep Him from
His right, it will matter not by what competitor.[1]
— William Wilberforce

There are times in every Christian's life when crisis requires a choice. As faith mellows and matures, successive seasons provoke climatic changes, spurring spiritual growth. Circumstances converge, collide, and crash together, placing us in a pivotal position in which familiar ways of coping and being comforted by a companion or counselor are gone.

A sudden job relocation, financial crisis, loss of a loved one, or some other unexpected trauma hits, and quick as a flash, we are heaved from the well-worn container of our former way of life into the grinding tumult of an unplanned-for existence.

"I never thought when I married Michael that we wouldn't have a good marriage," Anne, a thirty-four-year-old physician's wife, shared with me over coffee one evening, "but he started sleeping with a close friend of mine when I was pregnant with Cara.

"I realized that something had gone terribly wrong," said Anne. "I went numb. I became depressed. I felt wrecked. I couldn't imagine what my life would be like without Michael, partly because I knew that if I left him, even temporarily, it would also mean leaving a comfortable lifestyle I enjoy." Extensive professional and pastoral counseling — and many months of prayer — followed.

A few years later, Anne encountered a new challenge: Michael was involved in another long-term affair. This time, he was no longer interested in attending counseling or church and requested that Anne stop going too.

Things like this are not supposed to happen in committed Christians' lives. But they do.

My friend Rosemary met her moment of decision while lying on a hospital bed, awaiting surgery. When a pregnancy test had come back positive several weeks earlier, no one advocated that she carry the baby to term. Rosemary's husband threatened to leave her if she did not have an abortion; her pastor reasoned that she was too medically fragile to have the baby and advised she do the same; her doctor frightened her with a batch of alarming statistics and said that, at least from his perspective, any other course of action than his performing a full D&C procedure would be tantamount to malpractice.

The concept of "choice" was far from Rosemary's mind as she struggled with the life-and-death challenges imposed by her health condition. Looking up at the ceiling in her semiprivate room, she found herself praying for direction: *Something isn't right ... I feel good about the baby, God ... but what else can I do?*

~: :~

Significant turning points also occur in more subtle ways. Joan's crisis came after she went to a women's retreat on a summer weekend at a friend's church. Something the speaker had said kept going through her mind: "I challenge you to live for Christ in every area of life — to lay your private miseries at His feet, your heavy secrets at the foot of the cross — and to choose obedience to God over acceptance of sin."

What the speaker did not know was that Joan had been living with her boyfriend part-time while she was away at college. In fact, nobody back home knew about it, including the friend who had invited Joan to the retreat.

Summer vacation brought a reprieve from the inner conflict she had experienced earlier in the year concerning the relationship, but as the time to return to school grew closer, Joan found herself repeatedly going over the speaker's words. Was God trying to tell her something? And did she want to hear it?

Although Anne's marital circumstances, Rosemary's medical emergency, and Joan's confrontation with the Holy Spirit seem unrelated on the surface, their underlying struggle was surprisingly similar: None of them felt ready to take the next step toward God because it meant taking a step away from someone they deeply cared about. In cases of divided loyalties, a spiritual crisis such as these women experienced becomes a fork in the road, a place of deliberate decision-making, where two questions on an imaginary signpost highlight a clearly marked junction point: Whom will you follow? Which way will you go?

The grace of obedience — the single-minded selection of the Lord's will over our own preferences — brings us the courage to take the tough route. It protects our hearts and preserves us from harm, enabling us in faith to follow God's Word. "Which of you fears the Lord and obeys his servant's commands? The man who walks in dark places with no light, yet trusts in the name of the Lord and leans on his God" (Isa. 50:10 NEB).

Obedience keeps on the right course. Even in the darkness.

In Abigail's story, obedience required travel along a risky route on a secret life-saving mission. How could she have known where her decision to obey Israel's chosen king would eventually lead her?

Abigail's Story

~· 🍇 ·~

bigail was a woman at a crossroads. In the Old Testament we encounter Abigail, the wife of a fabulously wealthy Middle Eastern magnate named Nabal—a wise beauty wed to a willful beast of a man. Her obstinate husband, a Calebite, is described as being "surly and mean in his dealings" (1 Sam. 25:3). And he drank too much.

When we meet this sweet-and-sour couple in the Syrian desert, it is in the midst of the sheepshearing season. David, a former shepherd and the newly anointed king, has set up camp near Nabal's vast herds following the death of Samuel, the high priest. Following the local customs at shearing time, King David sends ten young men to bear a "Shalom" greeting of goodwill on his behalf to the affluent landowner. "Long life to you! Good health to you and your household! And good health to all that is yours!" proclaims the salutation.

"When your shepherds were with us, we did not mistreat them. . . . nothing of theirs was missing. Ask your servants and they will tell you. Therefore be favorable toward my young men, since we come at a festive time," the message entreats. "Please give your servants and your son David whatever you can find for them" (1 Sam. 25:5–8).

Responding with defiance, Nabal, whose name in Hebrew literally means "fool," arrogantly sneers: "Who is this David? Who is this son of Jesse? Many servants are breaking away from their masters these days. Why should I take my bread and water, and the meat I have slaughtered for my shearers, and give it to men coming from who knows where?" (1 Sam. 25:10–11). Although it was a matter of routine to dispatch a polite reply even to a man's deadliest enemy in such circumstances, Nabal apparently could not have cared less, making his uncouth remarks about the king even more insulting.

It does not take a genius to figure out what happens next. David, to put it mildly, is a fighting man. A proven giant-killer. A fully armed and loaded lethal weapon. A heroic he-man of a holy warrior — the kind of authentic action figure Hollywood tries to dream up, then makes billions of dollars trying to copy.

When news of Nabal's scorn reaches the king's camp, David shouts, "Put on your swords!" (1 Sam. 25:13). Under orders from the king, four hundred men start marching toward Nabal's wilderness compound.

Meanwhile, back at the ranch, one of Nabal's appropriately alarmed servants tells Abigail in colorful detail about what has happened. Now Nabal's wife is a smart woman. She thinks fast and moves cautiously. Abigail must know about David's legendary military status; she is also familiar with the king's generous treatment of Nabal's hired hands in the grazing fields; and, let us not forget, this veteran denizen of the desert understands her husband very well. So what does she decide to do?

Abigail immediately takes action to prevent bloodshed and disaster — without her husband's advice or consent.

Prepared for Action

Do not those who plot evil go astray? But those who plan what is good find love and faithfulness. Proverbs 14:22

Abigail's unusual choice is not presented here as a portrait of diabolical defiance. One has only to read a few lines farther down the page to discover that this remarkable woman is as gentle and gracious as she is strategically sound. But Abigail's loyal determination to obey the king was outrageously risky given her wifely status in the Middle East. Stern protocols undoubtedly stipulated a stiff sentence for her behavior; the consequences of her actions were likely to have involved brutal punishment; regardless of the outcome, she must have known from the moment she made this decision that her life would change dramatically.

Centuries later, people like Abigail would be called martyrs for taking similar risks and paying the price of their obedience to their King.

The scene we are left with is this: In the apparent absence of immediate, godly counsel, Abigail chooses to perform her domestic duty in an exceptional way, avoiding both inert terror and hand-wringing helplessness. Upon hearing about the disaster threatening her household, she sets out without delay to make peace, and courageously directs all of her energies toward helping the very man it would have been easiest for her to despise — her husband. Without consulting anyone, she secretly directs Nabal's servants to quickly put together an elaborate royal feast, enough to feed six hundred hungry men, to be carried at once on a fleet of donkeys to the king's camp (1 Sam. 25:18–19).

Can you imagine instantly whipping up an equivalent Thanksgiving meal of, say, sixty smoked turkeys, one hundred dozen yeast rolls, twenty-five pounds of butter, three hundred pounds of mashed potatoes, twenty gallons of gravy, fifty fruitcakes, and two hundred assorted pies, then transporting the entire assemblage miles out of town without your husband's even knowing about it?

Perhaps, if his life depended on it, you can.

Securing the King's Pardon

When pride comes, then comes disgrace, but with humility comes wisdom. Proverbs 11:2

Just as David swears to utterly destroy Nabal and all of his men — which, had this happened, would have left the women and their children open to all manner of attack and adversity — Abigail rides over the hill, and in a classic picture of perfect timing, blesses David and presents her impressive load of culinary delights.

The king immediately thanks God for intervening through Abigail's providential surprise.

"Praise be to the LORD, who has sent you today to meet me. May you be blessed for your good judgment and for keeping me from bloodshed this day and from avenging myself with my own hands," says the contrite king. "Otherwise, as surely as the LORD, the God of Israel lives, who has kept me from harming you, if you had not come quickly to meet me, not one male belonging to Nabal would have been left alive by daybreak" (1 Sam. 25:32–34).

Many years later, Jesus proclaimed: "Blessed are the peacemakers, for they will be called sons of God" (Matt. 5:9). Abigail, a Carmelite woman living in the Desert of Maon long before the Messiah's birth, was this kind of a peacemaker. Yet there are those who question the wisdom of her speedy actions. They wonder whether Abigail preempted God by intruding where she did not belong. They say that she was not a submissive wife because she bypassed her husband's oversight and approval, and they invalidate her perceptive courage.

But the king's affirmation of her hazardous service to the God of Israel says something else. And although it is impossible to know her innermost thoughts and true motives, Abigail appears to have properly feared God and Israel's appointed king more than she feared her cantankerous husband. Would the biblical record portray her as wise or show her in a favorable light if this had not been the case? Surely, the meeting with David presents Abigail as a remarkable example of humility, service, and obedience before her king.

When the question of divided loyalties arises, whom will we follow? Which way will we go?

A Costly Choice

The name of the LORD is a strong tower; the
righteous run to it and are safe. Proverbs 18:10

*E*xtraordinary afflictions are not always the punishment of extraordinary sins but the trial of extraordinary graces," Matthew Henry once observed. "Sanctified afflictions are spiritual promotions."[2]

Surely this was true for Abigail, who returns home to find Nabal feasting and drinking, apparently in oblivion to his peril, perhaps even in opposition to the king. A woman accustomed to a spouse's heavy drinking knows better than to invite intoxicated trouble, and so Abigail wisely waits to tell her husband what has happened.

The next morning, when he is sober and presumably recovering from a head-splitting hangover, Abigail presents Nabal with the news of her meeting with David. It is the last thing she ever says to him. Hit suddenly with heart failure and subsequent paralysis, the Scriptures say that the Lord "struck Nabal and he died" ten days later (1 Sam. 25:38).

Hearing of Nabal's rapid demise, David once again praises God for recognizing his cause and preventing vengeful violence. Many years later, David's son, Solomon, would write, "The Lord pulls down the proud man's house but he keeps the widow's boundaries intact" (Prov. 15:25) — a fitting proverb for Abigail, who joins the king's household after receiving a proposal of marriage by courier from David. Calamity changes into celebration. Abigail, the fool's widow, becomes the wife of the king.

For a woman of faith who finds herself in a relationship with a man in rebellion against God, peacemaking is sometimes thought to mean avoiding confrontations, burying the truth, and smiling through the pain. But through Abigail's valiant witness, we see faithfulness and obedience to the king rewarded. Clearly, staying silent is not always what God directs a woman to do.

Susanna's Story

~: 🍇 :~

"There once lived in Babylon a man named Joakim. . . ."
Introduced to us through this timeless literary opening,
we catch our first glimpse of Susanna, a wealthy family's daughter, in the Apocryphal Book of Susanna.

The wife of a very rich and influential Jew named Joakim,
Susanna is a stunningly beautiful woman. Her expansive home,
with its fine gardens, plentiful servants, and abundant amenities,
is a busy hub of social and religious activity in ancient Babylon,
where it serves as the spiritual center and courthouse of the
Hebrew community.

In this opulent setting, we also meet two recently appointed
judges who were previously elders; they are often at Joakim's
house due to the numerous trials taking place there. We are told in
a prophecy that wickedness will come forth among God's people
in Babylon through these men. Here is how it happens. Every day
at noon, when a regularly appointed recess sends people from the
house, Susanna spends her midday break time strolling in
Joakim's garden. Again and again, the two elders view the scene
from their separate vantage points, looking on with passionate
interest as Susanna enters her private paradise.

Eventually the men become so obsessed with lust for the gor-
geous woman that they no longer quite remember who they are or
what they believe in. Imaginary scenarios, forbidden fantasies, and
incessant plotting take hold of their minds. We are told: "They no
longer prayed to God, but let their thoughts stray from him and
forgot the claims of morality. They were both infatuated with her;
but they did not tell each other what pangs they suffered, because
they were ashamed to confess that they wanted to seduce her. Day
after day they watched eagerly to see her" (Sus. 1:9–12 NEB).

Time passes. A fiery desire consumes the judges' common
sense as their consciences are slowly seared. Then one day, as each

man catches the other spying on Susanna, the legal experts unexpectedly find themselves face-to-face with their mutual secret.

Alone But Not Defenseless

*The heart of the righteous weighs its answers, but the
mouth of the wicked gushes evil.* Proverbs 15:28

*T*he men can find no reasonable excuse to use as a defense, and after answering one another's questions, each confesses his dark passion to the other. But rather than wisely renouncing their reckless behavior and repenting of their sexual obsession for Susanna, they conspire to join forces. Deciding to commit their crime against her together, they agree to meet frequently until they find the woman alone, and they begin to look for an opportunity to seduce her.

Unaware of the illicit attention she is receiving, Susanna decides one day to bathe in the garden. After sending her servant away to bring back soap and olive oil, the co-conspirators, who are silently watching as they hide nearby, realize that Susanna's privacy is assured.

As soon as the maid leaves, the elders spring out of the thick greenery and reveal their intent, pointing out the obvious truth to the stunned woman: The garden doors are shut, no one is available to act as a witness, and they will serve as Susanna's judges if any charges are brought before the court. "We are burning for desire for you, so consent and yield to us," they demand. "If you refuse, we shall give evidence against you that there was a young man with you and that was why you sent your maid away" (Sus. 1:21).

Groaning, Susanna realizes that she is trapped, and with a cry of anguish announces, "I see no way out" (Sus. 1:22). Yet the scene does not end here. Under tremendous pressure, Susanna promptly considers her options and chooses to obey God.

"If I do this thing, the penalty is death; if I do not, you will have me at your mercy," she reasons. With firm resolve, she declares her final decision: "My choice is made: I will not do it. It is better to be at your mercy than to sin against the Lord" (Sus. 1:22–23).

Then Joakim's faithful wife screams for help at the top of her lungs.

The elders do not lose a second recouping their advantage. When Susanna gives a loud shout, they shout louder. One of the judges rushes to open the garden door, perhaps to make it appear as if he is chasing Susanna's supposed lover, as servants stream through the gate. After hearing the elders' steamy version of the story, the listeners stand by in a state of shock.

Will they believe the respected judicial representatives standing before them, or their kind mistress, whose impeccable reputation simply does not line up with the men's scandalous accusations?

Looking Toward Heaven

The fear of the LORD is a fountain of life, turning a man from the snares of death. Proverbs 14:27

The following day, Susanna is brought before the court, surrounded by family, friends, court representatives, and other members of her close-knit community. If the judges are successful in presenting and trying their case — and everyone present is painfully aware of this — humiliation and death will be the prescribed penalty.

A private, sensitive woman, Susanna is closely veiled as she faces her accusers. The elders order the veil removed: They cannot resist feasting their eyes upon her radiant face one more time. In doing this, the cunning judges also associate additional shame and scandal with the accused defendant. Weeping is heard around the room. Susanna's parents and children watch as the two men place their hands on her silky hair and then deliver their twisted testimony.

Listening silently, Susanna looks "up to heaven through her tears" (Sus. 1:35), and continues to trust God. Again, the evidence is presented; again, there appears to be no way out.

The assembly believes the treacherous judges and unjustly condemns Susanna to death.

With a plaintive cry for mercy, the blameless woman boldly directs her petition to a higher court in an unseen realm: "Eternal God, who dost know all secrets and foresee all things, thou knowest that their evidence against me was false. And now I am to die, guiltless though I am of all the wicked things these men have said against me" (Sus. 1:42–43).

The Lord hears Susanna's cry. As she is led out of the courtroom to her execution, God inspires someone in the crowd to protest. "I will not have this woman's blood upon my head!" (Sus. 1:46), he shouts with supernatural authority, and in a moment of high drama, a young prophet named Daniel boldly steps forward to defend the righteous woman's dignity before the court, demanding that the trial be reopened.

Truth and Freedom

Acquitting the guilty and condemning the innocent —
the LORD detests them both. Proverbs 17:15

$\mathcal{A}$s the gathering of people returns hurriedly to the courtroom, they are led by a group of elders who have been silent up to this point. Asking Daniel to assume a place among them, the assembled leaders quickly discern the source of his inspired intervention and submit straightway to his direction.

"Separate these men and keep them at a distance from each other," he says firmly to the surprised advisors, "and I will examine them" (Sus. 1:51).

It becomes immediately evident that God has granted special insight to Daniel about the two judges' dealings. How else could he possibly know about all the other occasions when they have given unjust decisions, condemned the innocent, and acquitted the guilty in defiance of God's law? In what other way would he be able to tell that the elders had been lying all along?

In the end, a simple question turns up the truth. "If you saw this woman, tell us, under what tree did you see them together?" Daniel inquires (Sus. 1:53). When the two men supply conflicting testimony, Daniel triumphantly proves Susanna's innocence. The people give a great shout, praising God; the judges are executed in an innocent woman's place; and Susanna's family gives thanks for their loved one's refusal to submit to the elders' evil scheme.

Consequently, by the incredible story's dramatic conclusion, a consistent contrast in character between Susanna's purity and the judges' vileness emerges: Honesty denounces deceit; righteousness faces hypocrisy; trust defeats doubt; courage conquers cowardice; and humility overrules pride.

"Obedience must be the struggle and desire of our life," observed the nineteenth-century hymn writer Phillips Brooks. "Obedience, not hard and forced but ready, loving and spontaneous; the doing of duty, not merely that the duty may be done, but that the soul in doing it may become capable of receiving and uttering God."[3] Through Susanna's story, the truth of this statement leaps into view through the actions of an obedient woman who was willing to stand alone — devalued, degraded, and apparently disbelieved by even her dearest companions — in the presence of her Lord. She exhibited no fear concerning what the judges might do to her; she feared her eternal Judge instead. Repelling the aggressors' advances, she refused to disregard the law she loved or compromise her integrity, resisting their destructive duplicity with all her strength.

Like Abigail, Susanna acted wisely without the benefit of human comfort, counsel, or companionship. Her quick decisions were a matter of conviction, not coercion. She did not automatically align herself with the authorities who consciously rebelled against God. And she was not afraid to follow the righteous path.

Did Susanna ever imagine that her miraculous deliverance would come through an unknown prophet waiting in the crowd? Or did she just assume that her decision was a death sentence? We do not know. It is only in retrospect that we see the glorious outcome of her obedience: With God's help, Susanna's choice saved her life.

⌒ 🍇 ⌒

Be Thou my vision, O Lord of my heart;
Naught be all else to me save that Thou art —
Thou my best thought, by day or by night,
Waking or sleeping, Thy presence my light.
Be Thou my Wisdom, and Thou my true Word;
I ever with Thee and Thou with me, Lord;
Thou my great Father, I Thy true son,
Thou in me dwelling, and I with Thee one.
Be Thou my Breastplate, my Sword for the fight;
Be Thou my Armor, and be Thou my might;
Thou my sole Shelter, and Thou my high Tower —
Raise Thou me heavenward, O Power of my power.
Riches I heed not, nor man's empty praise,
Thou mine inheritance, now and always.
Thou and Thou only, first in my heart,
High King of heaven, my Treasure Thou art.
High King of heaven, my victory won,
May I reach heaven's joys, O bright heaven's Sun!
Heart of my own heart, whatever befall,
Still be my Vision, O Ruler of all.

—Ancient Irish hymn,
trans. by Mary E. Byrne

CONCLUSION

When faced with compromising our commitment to Christ, let us recall the stories of Abigail and Susanna. We can trust God, as they did, to meet us at our point of need.

As He guided Abigail on her strenuous peacekeeping mission and responded to Susanna's last-minute plea for mercy, our heavenly Father also reveals to us the right path to take. We can choose to follow where His directions point even when those around us — valued co-workers, casual acquaintances, respected clergy, extended family, close companions — get sidetracked or lose their way in the darkness. We can decide to turn away from dead-end pursuits toward the reality of our redemption.

Once-in-a-lifetime declarations of our commitment are not enough. Periodic checks are also needed to discover our current ruler's identity. Who is seated on the throne of our lives? Is it self — or Christ the King?

Obedience to God places the rightful Ruler on His throne and puts the self at risk. Abigail placed herself in tremendous peril when she chose to make peace with her king; she could not have possibly predicted the final turn of events following her decision to carry a meal to David. Susanna, making her pivotal decision while cornered in a private garden, was unaware of God's upcoming intervention on her behalf through a prophet.

But following the Lord's commands is more than dutiful doing. Through actively walking with God, we are conformed to His will; and as we walk, our faith to follow Him increases. By freely responding to the grace of obedience with our whole hearts, we enter a new realm of trust in God.

"Obedience is rooted in love, not fear; it is activated by affection, not by force. Keeping the commandments, for Christians," Eugene Peterson reminds us, "is not dull rule-keeping but passionate love-making: Each commandment is a channel for expressing and sharing God's goodness."[4]

How much we need to hear and heed the Lord's promise that He will light our way with His love and grace and protection — to know that our Father in heaven loves us even when we resist His holy intervention; to understand that His commands are for our good, lighting the way ahead; to yield to His grace and be sustained by His Spirit.

"If you love me, you will obey what I command," said Jesus to His disciples (John 14:15). Yet the Lord did not end there. He said something more: "And I will ask the Father and he will give you another Counselor to be with you forever — the Spirit of truth. The world cannot accept him, because it neither sees him nor knows him. But you know him, for he lives with you and will be in you. I will not leave you as orphans; I will come to you" (John 14:16–18).

Unlike Abigail and Susanna, we are not alone along the rugged road of obedience — we have the Lord's Spirit to lead us in the way of truth. A lasting source of comfort and joy — the dynamic, indwelling presence of God's supernatural strength. God is with us!

"The word *Comforter* as applied to the Holy Spirit needs to be translated by some vigorous terms," emphasizes E. Paul Hovey. "Literally, it means 'with strength.' Jesus promised His followers that 'The Strengthener' would be with them forever. This promise is no lullaby for the fainthearted. It is a blood transfusion for courageous living."[5]

The Strengthener. I like that expression, don't you? Especially on days when I am tempted to stop resisting sin and simply give in. When my imperfection and weakness threaten to overwhelm me. Or even when the laundry piles up, the car with 82,000 miles on it needs new brakes, and a dental visit is the next thing on my schedule.

"To learn sense is true self-love," wrote Solomon (Prov. 19:8 NEB). Will we "learn sense" as the wise king advised and seek the Spirit's help in times of stress and crisis? When presented with the choice of obedience, on whose strength will we depend?

Points for Reflection

1. I am encouraged to obey God most when I . . .
2. It is especially easy to forget to put my trust in the Lord if . . .
3. Abigail's obedience to the king makes me think that . . .
4. The Holy Spirit's strength has been especially evident in my life when . . .
5. I will be reminded of Susanna's story the next time I am faced with . . .
6. Jesus' chief competitor to ruling on my heart's throne is . . .

Prayer: Dear Jesus, save me from self-rule. Place my feet on the righteous path. Fill me with Your life, O Lord, as I obediently place my trust in You. Revive my desire to remain in Your love as I rely on Your strength instead of my own. In Your name, I ask. Amen.

⌣ 🍇 ⌢

LORD, you have assigned me my portion and
my cup;
you have made my lot secure.
The boundary lines have fallen for me in
pleasant places;
surely I have a delightful inheritance.
I will praise the LORD who counsels me;
even at night my heart instructs me.
I have set the LORD always before me.
Because he is at my right hand,
I will not be shaken.
Therefore my heart is glad and my tongue
rejoices;
my body also will rest secure,
because you will not abandon me to the grave,
nor will you let your Holy One see decay.
You have made known to me the path of life;
you will fill me with joy in your presence,
with eternal pleasures at your right hand.

— Psalm 16:5–11

In every heart He wishes to be first:
He therefore keeps the secret key Himself
To open all its chambers, and to bless,
With perfect sympathy and holy peace,
Each solitary soul which comes to Him.

— Anonymous

Chapter Five

Devotion

It is love that asks, that seeks, that knocks, that finds,
and that is faithful to what it finds.[1]

— St. Augustine

*H*as anyone ever suggested that you are "wasting" your time and talents on following Christ? Have you ever wondered about this yourself?

At a time when words like *burnout* and *codependency* are a common part of many people's vocabularies, the expression *true devotion* has an implicitly high-risk, watch-out-this-is-bad-for-you, unwritten warning attached to it. Like a cheese-covered, triple-egg omelet loaded with guacamole, chopped olives, and sour cream, some believe that devotion is to be indulged in only occasionally, with proper restraint, in limited portions. And for good reason: Living a self-denying, performance-oriented life in order to prove one's worthiness and lovability to God is, to put it quite simply, harmful for one's spiritual health.

But the grace of devotion is different. When we see devotion as a gift of God, supplied to bless and encourage our union with Christ, we know that it is not something we can conjure up on our own, independent from the Holy Spirit's loving assistance. It is not based on our calculated attempts to impress the Lord. Far from it: The grace of devotion frees us to express our love for Jesus without fear and worry and keeps us close to the Lord's feet.

Everyone is devoted, to a greater or lesser extent, to whatever or whomever they genuinely love and admire — a spouse, their ministry, an enviable job, staying fit, or maintaining a certain standard of living. But competing demands placed on our talents, energy, and financial resources, combined with our natural desire for reward and recognition, distract our devotion away from Christ. And rather than regularly waiting on the Holy Spirit to revive our devotion, we are prone to rushing ahead to the next thing on the agenda that needs our attention. Quiet times with Jesus get put on indefinite hold; before long, we become confused about God's calling and begin to wonder whether we've made the best choices.

✧ ✧

Barbra recently returned to Illinois from the mission field in Brazil after spending more than a decade planting churches there. Not surprisingly, reentry into North American life is proving difficult. "When I look around and see what my friends have acquired and accomplished over the past fifteen years," shares my middle-aged friend, "I definitely feel left behind and out of the mainstream. I just turned forty, yet we still don't own a home or have health insurance — things many people our age take for granted. I find myself wanting these things too.

"It's really hard to accept that we're at about the same point as many couples in their early twenties, at least in terms of financial security and material possessions," Barbra says.

As she considers how her life might have been if she had established a secular career in the States, self-doubt creeps in. *What about my needs and desires? If we had done things differently, I could be living in my own house by now instead of renting again. How many more times will we have to move before we finally settle down?*

✧ ✧

When she was single and in her late twenties, Julie worked in China, teaching English as a second language to university students. She told me in her letters about the harsh conditions, greasy food, and dismal climate that she encountered after her arrival, and sometimes wrote about the difficulties she faced while sharing the Gospel in a hostile environment.

I recall Julie's sharing, "Building relationships with the students that will allow me to be open about my faith with them is going to take a long time. I'm praying for the wisdom, and patience, to do this in a way that's sensitive to the Holy Spirit. I really don't know how many of them I'll be able to reach while I'm here. For now, my work in the classroom must be my only witness. It's turning out so differently from what I expected."

In light of her frustrating circumstances, Julie sometimes speculated: *Am I where You want me to be, Lord? Sometimes I think I'm probably missing the best moments of my life by continuing to work here. I can't see any obvious outcomes. I miss my friends and family. I feel lonely a lot of the time. Is this worth it?*

᠁ ᠁

Lynn's children had almost completed high school when she applied to a graduate program in preparation for the years ahead. Carefully calculating the time it would take before she began working full time as an attorney, she counted on being in law school for three years, followed by intensive study prior to taking the state bar exam, before reaching her goal.

"I've been wanting to do this for so long," Lynn told me a few months ago. "When the kids were little, I thought it was going to take forever to get to this point. Now that I've finally arrived at my destination, I'm no longer sure if practicing law is what I want to spend the rest of my life doing."

Her internal struggle sounded familiar to me as she recounted: "I keep thinking back to the way I was when I first met the Lord. Remember those prayer meetings we used to have, how naive we all were? Oh, did we ever do some ridiculous things! Yet, I can't help but wonder if God is calling me to a similar spot. Is getting my J.D. degree really what the Lord wants me to do next?"

᠁ ᠁

"Woman's life today," writes Anne Morrow Lindbergh in *Gift from the Sea*, "is tending more and more toward . . . 'torn-to-pieces-hood.'"[2] The hectic pace many of us — my friends, I, and maybe, you — so easily fall into demands constant reevaluation. From the perspective of our contemporary culture, if we hope to achieve anything of real "value," we must meet certain expectations, adopt specific attitudes, and always look our best — regardless of what it costs. We must get out there and fight to win — to combat fat, bait a mate, impress the boss, buy the best, dress for success — in a constant struggle to promote ourselves and our personal programs. Never mind if we happen to encounter family breakdown, bulimia, clinical depression, or a heart attack along the way.

But this has little to do with what Jesus taught.

"The kingdom of God is a kingdom of paradox, where through the ugly defeat of the cross a holy God is utterly glorified," Charles Colson reminds us in *Loving God*. "Victory comes through defeat; healing through brokenness; finding self through losing self."[3] Speaking from a biblical standpoint, Colson's statement brings us back to this inescapable reality: The things of this world — the bent of our present culture — are at war with the kingdom of heaven. If we are fighting to win, on which side are we fighting? To whom are our hearts most devoted?

Mary of Bethany is an example of someone whose spiritual devotion Jesus admired and approved of. To many, Mary's story might sound like a wasted life — perhaps even an easy one. And yet, among Christ's followers, she was the only person whom Jesus commended on three strikingly dissimilar occasions.

Mary of Bethany's Story

~: 🍇 :~

With the exception of Jesus, no one could have guessed what Mary was about to do. Moving past the guests at the dinner party, she shattered the alabaster box and spilled the precious perfume over the Master's head.

Small white chips sprinkled the hem of her brightly colored dress as the fragrance of the nard hit each witness full force — a clearly unforgettable odor, reminiscent of harems and funeral processions. Outraged, Judas angrily complained, "Why this waste? The perfume might have been sold for fifty dollars and the money given to the poor. It was worth a whole year's wages!" (Mark 14:5 NEB; John 12:5) He did not actually care about the poor; he was a thief and often pilfered cash from the disciple's money bag.

Along with Judas, several others suddenly turned in fury upon the kneeling woman. Facing her Savior, Mary fastened her eyes on Jesus only. Nothing else she had ever done compared to this extravagant demonstration of love.

Had she done something wrong?

Then Jesus started speaking. "Leave her alone," He demanded. "Why are you bothering her? She has done a beautiful thing to me" (Mark 14:6). Sometime later, Judas left with a plan to betray God's Son for thirty pieces of silver.

Imagine what it would be like to be Mary as you give your most valuable treasure to Christ. Suppose your sacrifice dramatically diminishes your financial strength — perhaps to the point of poverty. Picture your friends' furious protest as the precious possession is quickly used up and discarded, apparently for no "higher" purpose than to honor Jesus.

Within days of the event, when your beloved Teacher is betrayed by the man who was most enraged by your action, do you think you might find it difficult to believe that Jesus' imprisonment has nothing to do with your controversial behavior? If it were not for the Lord's open approval of your heartfelt sacrifice, how else would you know you had done the right thing?

Did Mary of Bethany know? Or were the days following Jesus' visit, filled with trouble and turmoil for even His most loyal disciples, confusing for Mary as well? What was her life like during that cataclysmic cluster of days?

The One Thing

Again, the kingdom of heaven is like a merchant looking for fine pearls. When he found one of great value, he went away and sold everything he had and bought it. Matthew 13:45–46

We do not know what happened to Mary after the Last Supper, for she is never mentioned in the Gospels again. But looking back from the vantage point of that evening, the apostles' accounts of her interactions with the Lord place her in a unique category. What was it about this particular follower of the Lord that made her so extraordinary?

The New Testament tells us nothing of her regular work or later ministry and offers no clues about her physical appearance. Her occupation and looks were of no real importance to the One who saw her heart. As we ponder the meaning of the "beautiful sacrifice" that Jesus promised would be shared in Mary's memory throughout the world, what do we see?

"She did what she could," is the way Jesus expressed it (Mark 14:8).

As we watch Mary in this scene, she does not dismiss her desire to anoint Jesus as wasteful, nor does she wait for a "perfect" time to act. In a spirit of love and worship, she seizes the moment with what is at hand, immediately setting her apart from those who measure their gifts to God by cost-benefit analysis. She infuriates several disciples at Simon's home. But her lavish sacrifice is highly praised by the Lord. And, regardless of what anyone else may say, His opinion is the one that counts.

On another occasion, Mary's sister, Martha, opens her home to the Lord and His disciples as they travel through the village of

Bethany. While busily preparing dinner for the group, she becomes frustrated by the situation and freely voices her concerns.

"Lord, don't you care that my sister has left me to do all the work by myself?" Martha says with foot-stomping aggravation, obviously overwhelmed. "Tell her to help me!" (Luke 10:40).

Martha, no doubt, is sincerely going about her business when she finally reaches her stress limit. But Jesus does not offer her His sympathy; He offers a kind rebuke instead. Without flinching, He gently replies, "Martha, Martha, you are worried and upset about many things, but only one thing is needed. Mary has chosen what is better, and it will not be taken away from her" (Luke 10:41–42).

Meanwhile, there is Mary, sitting at Jesus' feet, seemingly oblivious to her sister's hectic serving schedule, waiting for the Lord to resume instructing the disciples. Once again, her behavior is unconventional (it would have been unusual for a woman of that day to sit with men and listen to a rabbi's teaching) as she goes against the grain of social expectations; once again, Jesus commends Mary's perceptive choice and tenderly reproves Martha for placing her daily cares in a position of greater importance than spending time with Him.

"Lord, If You Had Been Here..."

The kingdom of heaven is like a mustard seed, which a man took and planted in his field. Though it is the smallest of all your seeds, it is the largest of the garden plants and becomes a tree, so that the birds of the air come and perch in its branches. Matthew 13:31–32

At Lazarus's tomb, Martha's intelligent self-sufficiency clashes against Mary's "frivolous" responsiveness to Christ's love once again. Though the two grieving women greet Jesus with the same words, they do so at separate times, in different ways.

Seeing the Lord for the first time after their brother's death, they say simply: "Lord, if you had been here, my brother would not have died" (John 11:21–32).

But there is a world of difference in what follows their faith statements. The words are identical, but the meanings behind them clearly do not match. As we read the passage slowly, from beginning to end (John 11:1–45), and compare Jesus' reactions to the two sisters, we can tell that He loves them both, and yet, to whom does He respond with tears? To Mary—who brings her broken heart to Jesus as a sacrifice, laying her grief out before the Lord in all its devastating agony.

If any doubt remains about the difference between Martha and Mary's approach toward Jesus after this encounter, we are given one more glimpse at the two women's hearts in this passage, just before Lazarus is raised from the dead. After arriving at the tomb, the Lord orders the stone to be rolled away from the cave's entrance. But then there is a pause.

Among all the people present, who is protesting Jesus' command?

Martha is. Voicing her clear opposition from a commonsense standpoint, the dead man's shocked sister self-assuredly protests, "But, Lord, he has been dead four days. By this time he will be decaying . . ." (John 11:39 PHILLIPS).

In reply to Martha's logical alarm, Jesus answers bluntly: "Did I not tell you that if you believed, you would see the wonder of what the Lord can do?" (John 11:40, PHILLIPS).

Some claim that Mary of Bethany was the "sensual" sister of the two, an out-of-touch dreamer whose personality somehow led her to go to emotional extremes. But as we study every passage in which she appears (Mark 14:3–9; Luke 10:38–42; John 11:1–45; 12:1–8), her witness demonstrates something else: the lasting testimony of a believing disciple.

When she discovered heaven's greatest treasure, Mary's devotion came into focus. And, upon finding the love of her life, she did what she could to buy the field, purchase the pearl, and bury faith's tiny mustard seed in the fertile furrows of her faithful, trusting heart.

Mary's Defender

The kingdom of heaven is like treasure hidden in a field. When a man found it, he hid it again, and then in his joy went and sold all he had and bought that field. Matthew 13:44

*D*evotion to our Creator and King can take many forms as we gratefully recognize God's absolute holiness and divinity. As Martha discovered, stress, strife, and resentment result from trying to self-sufficiently love and serve others. Why not try taking a thirst-quenching drink at the wellspring's source instead?

Remember David's act of worship as he "danced before the Lord with all his might" before the Ark of the Covenant as it was carried into Jerusalem? As she watched from a window, his wife, Michal, despised the nearly-naked David for leaping about the city streets in such an unkingly manner, in full view of his servants and subjects. Michal was concerned only with her husband's outward demeanor, but God saw David's heart, perhaps in much the same way that Jesus could see Mary of Bethany's heart.

The sacrifice of devotion, like David's and Mary's, runs counter to everything in us that prefers to exalt self above Jesus; thus, devotion can only arise from a willingness to take our eyes off ourselves — and our critics — and turn our thoughts toward God. We are no longer strangers to God's kingdom, but worship our holy King with the angels.

Paul wrote: "With eyes wide open to the mercies of God, I beg you, my brothers, as an act of intelligent worship, to give him your bodies, as a living sacrifice, consecrated to him and acceptable by him. Do not let the world around you squeeze you into its mold, but let God re-make you so that your whole attitude of mind is changed. Thus you will prove in practice that the will of God's good, acceptable to him and perfect" (Rom. 12:1–2 Phillips).

Mary's story is a grand encouragement for all believers in this regard. She did not seem to care about how it would "look" to sit at the Lord's feet as His disciple or anoint Jesus' head, pour expensive perfume over his feet, and wipe off the extra oil with her hair. Responding to the Holy Spirit, she acted appropriately, given the circumstances. And Jesus defended her sacrifice of love.

"Feed on Christ, and then go and live your life, and it is Christ in you that lives your life, that helps the poor, that tells the truth, that fights the battle, and that wins the crown," proclaimed Phillips Brooks.[4]

It is a lesson we never stop learning.

Teresa of Avila's Story

At first glimpse, Teresa de Cepeda y Ahumada, a self-confessed book lover, captivating conversationalist, and refreshingly honest Christian, might seem an unlikely candidate for canonized sainthood. But a closer look reveals the heart of a holy captive freely enjoying the peculiar sacrifice of a cloistered life.

Teresa was born on March 28, 1515, in Avila, an old Spanish town known for its religious tolerance and family lineage fervor. Few people knew that as a young boy, her father, Alonso de Cepeda, had been vigorously persecuted in Toledo with his Jewish family during the Spanish Inquisition in 1485, or that his father had changed the family's last name before relocating to Avila, where the Cepedas became professing Catholics. Whether they continued to privately practice Judaism remains unknown.

By the time Teresa joined the family, her father was a prominent tax collector and remarried widower; two children, a boy and a girl, had survived his first marriage. His second wife, Beatriz de Ahumada, was only nineteen when she gave birth to Teresa, her third child and first daughter. A quietly intelligent, beautiful young woman, the delicate Beatriz was severely weakened by frequent pregnancies; she died while giving birth to her ninth child when Teresa was nearly thirteen, leaving Don Alonso to oversee his large family alone.

Teresa spent these early years of her womanhood as a typical teenager, infatuated with clothes and romance. She especially adored the flattery and attention of her neighboring cousins. During this period, two significant events took place: The first, a secret encounter with a male relative living next door, she described as coming close to endangering the lives of her father and brothers, who would have been forced to defend her honor if things had gone much further; the second, not coincidentally, took place soon afterward, when the sixteen-year-old's father discreetly placed her in a Augustinian convent school, Our Lady of Grace.

"If I had to advise parents, I should tell them to take great care about the people with whom their children associate. . . . ," Teresa wrote many years later. "Much harm may result from bad company and we are inclined by nature to follow what is worse rather than better."[5]

The transition to cloistered life, which would have proved unbearably difficult for many girls her age, was surprisingly smooth. Within a week after her arrival at the school, the repentant young woman discovered she was far happier than she had been in her father's boisterous house. Tired of leading a spiritually impoverished life, Teresa was relieved when her friend's messages, which previously had been smuggled into the convent from the outside, suddenly stopped.

Building Blocks

> *Ask and it will be given to you; seek and you will find; knock and the door will be opened to you.* Matthew 7:7

*I*n the convent, Teresa rediscovered her roots. As a child, she had found great pleasure in learning about saints' lives, reading her mother's chivalric novels, and attempting to build small stone hermitages in the garden beside her favorite brother, Rodrigo, with whom she frequently discussed how they could achieve martyrdom. Once, they even set out together, Teresa says, "to go to the country of the Moors, begging our way for the love of God, that they might behead us there; and, even at so tender an age, I believe the Lord had given us sufficient courage for this, if we could have found a way to do it; but our greatest hindrance seemed to be that we had a father and a mother."[6] The two children reached Adaja, a town near Avila, before being retrieved by their uncle.

Her parents set a lasting example. According to Teresa, "It was a help to me that I never saw my parents inclined to anything but virtue."[7] From her father, Teresa acquired a lifelong appreciation for good literature, strict honesty, and temperate language; from her mother, the necessity of prayer and beauty of calm intelligence. In addition to his generosity toward the poor and compassion for the sick, Alonso adamantly refused to own slaves, and although she was a very beautiful woman, Beatriz never accentuated her fine figure with clothes or made the slightest reference to her appearance.

Looking back on her childhood many years later, Teresa openly acknowledged that among all of her father's children, she always believed herself to be the least virtuous and the most in need of improvement and often contemplated what it would be like to be a nun. As adolescence approached, her interest in such spiritual topics started to wane.

A teacher's companionship and the convent's reflective atmosphere, however, revived Teresa's interest in serving Christ. As she watched the nuns' reverent behavior, she regretted her heart's hardness and began to seek God's will regarding her future vocation. Yet the necessary peace of mind required to take the next step continually eluded her.

"I began to say a great many vocal prayers and to get all the nuns to commend me to God and pray that He would bring me to a state in which I was to serve Him," Teresa candidly confesses. "By the end of my time there, I was much more reconciled to being a nun — though not in that house, because of the very virtuous practices which I had come to hear that they observed and which seemed to me to be altogether excessive.... These good thoughts about being a nun came to me from time to time but they soon left me and I could not persuade myself to become one."[8]

At about this time, the young student fell sick, suffering from fainting spells and high fevers, and her father brought her back home. By the time her eighteen-month stay at the convent ended, though she still lacked clear direction concerning her calling, Teresa felt herself much improved.

For God's Sake Alone

But seek first his kingdom and his righteousness, and all these things will be given to you as well. Matthew 6:33

Slowly, Teresa's vocation became clearer. For a time, Teresa stayed at home, helping to raise her younger siblings — a family ministry that she was engaged in, to one degree or another, until she died. Inspired by the epistles of Saint Jerome, she began to find her calling irresistible and shared with her father her thoughts about becoming a nun.

Alonso refused to give his consent. As his favorite child, the most support Teresa was able to obtain from him was his permission to do as she liked after he passed away.

Troubled by her vulnerability to temptation and urged by inner fears that she might lapse in her devotion to Christ, Teresa left home in 1536 and secretly presented herself as a novice at the Convent of the Incarnation, where her close friend and mentor, Sister Jane Suarez, lived. Realizing that it was too late to dissuade his daughter, Teresa's father finally relented, and a year later, at the age of twenty-one, her confession as a Carmelite nun was secure. Initially, this new life brought Teresa great encouragement. She explains:

> Everything connected with the religious life caused me delight; and it is a fact that sometimes, when I was spending time sweeping floors which I had previously spent on my own indulgence and adornment and realized that I was now free from all those things, there came to me a new joy, which amazed me, for I could not understand whence it arose. Whenever I recall this, there is nothing, however hard, which I would not undertake if it were proposed to me. . . . I would never recommend anyone, when a good inspiration comes to him again and again, to hesitate to put it into practice because of fear; for if one lives a life of detachment for God's sake alone, there is no reason to be afraid that things will turn out amiss, since He is all-powerful.[9]

Although Teresa's happiness was great, the drastic change in her life and diet adversely affected her health. An illness, presumed to be malignant malaria, grew progressively worse. Accompanied by Sister Juarez, the newly pledged nun was forced to leave the convent for a period of three years.

Teresa's father arranged to send his sick daughter to a famous physician living near her married sister Maria's farm. While staying at her uncle Pedro's farm for a few days on the way to Maria's, the ailing nun received a batch of books from her devout uncle, including one called the *Spiritual Alphabet*, a treatise on quiet prayer. She could not stop reading it. The book provoked a historic turning point in Teresa's walk with God.

Through the Valley

For where your treasure is, there your heart will be also. Matthew 6:21

Periods of solitude, the "gift of tears," and the practice of quiet prayer introduced Teresa to a new realm of devotion to Jesus. Confined by illness, she made rapid progress in intimate communion with God, a providential preparation for the months of torturous therapies that lay ahead.

The aggressive medical treatments, which did much to increase her suffering, failed to alleviate the terrible affliction attacking Teresa's body. Day and night, rest eluded her. She fell into a deep coma and, in a state of paralysis, was believed to have perished.

As her attendants made plans for Teresa's burial, her father stubbornly refused to allow them to touch her body, repeatedly insisting, "The child isn't dead!" And he was right.

After four days, Teresa slowly opened her eyes, and deciding that she had endured enough of the physicians' bizarre assaults, asked to be returned to her convent — either to recover or die. Extremely weak and in great pain, eight months passed before Teresa could move. Another two years went by before she was able to crawl on her hands and knees. A few months later, she walked.

After three years of intense suffering, Teresa's physical health substantially returned, though her digestive system and heart had been permanently damaged during the ordeal. Full of gratitude and serious resolutions, Teresa nevertheless experienced a spiritual relapse:

> Who would have said that I would fall so soon, after receiving so many favors from God, and after His Majesty had begun to grant me virtues which themselves aroused me to fear Him; after I had seen myself at death's door . . . after He had raised me up, in soul and body, so that all who saw me were amazed to see me alive? What it is, my Lord, to have to live a life so full of perils! For here I am writing this, and it seems to me that with Thy favour and through Thy mercy I might say with Saint Paul, though not so perfectly as he: For it is not I now who live, but Thou, my Creator, livest in me.[10]

During her long convalescence, Teresa's inner strength had grown steadily through the long months of solitude and prayer, but upon her recovery, her genial surroundings provided unexpected enticements. More like a strictly run sorority house than a cloistered enclave, the convent's atmosphere tossed Teresa into troubled waters.

Since the convent's accommodations varied according to each nun's family dowry, Teresa was given an ample suite — two rooms, plus a kitchen — a comfortable living space that proved to be more conducive to socializing than solitude. Nuns frequently greeted visitors, including men, and the convent's 140 nuns were welcome to return home often to relieve burdensome living costs.

Thus, the good-humored beauty found herself facing the same spiritual detours she was the least able to bypass: light flirtations and lengthy conversations. Her witty charm, affectionate exuberance, and kind generosity were greatly appreciated by all — not least by the convent's visitors.

Lacking an instructor to guide her growth in prayer and distracted by these subtle daily temptations, Teresa made little solid spiritual progress over the next twenty years.

A Precious Sacrifice

> *If you, then, though you are evil, know how to give good gifts*
> *to your children, how much more will your Father in heaven*
> *give good gifts to those who ask him!* Matthew 7:11

A divided heart and mind kept Teresa in almost a constant state of frustration, or, as she explains it, in "one of the most grievous kinds of life which I think can be imagined, for I had neither any joy in God nor any pleasure in the world."[11] Eventually, the struggle became unbearable, and Teresa's spiritual development froze.

At the same time that Teresa's prayer life withered, her father's gained momentum. Noticing the change, Alonso avoided spending extended time with his daughter, who told him that ongoing health problems prevented her from praying as she had before. He fell ill and died while reciting a Catholic creed in 1543 after joyously embracing the same church that had subjected his family to cruel humiliations many years before.

Upon his death, Alonso's confessor, a Dominican friar named Francis, confronted the grieving nun about the dangerous rut she was in and gave her a copy of Augustine's *Confessions* to read. Seeing herself in its pages, with abundant tears Teresa resolved to devote herself wholly to the Lord from that time on and, at the determined friar's insistence, resumed the practice of quiet prayer and never again abandoned it.

Bit by bit, Teresa gained the courage to withdraw from intrusive pleasures and pursuits. "Dear God, what a soul suffers and what torments it endures when it loses its freedom to be its own master! I am astonished now that I was able to live in such a state of torment," Teresa exclaims in her autobiography. "God be praised, Who gave me life to forsake such utter death!"[12]

Gifted by God with the grace of contemplation, Teresa began to inwardly reflect upon Jesus in the Garden of Gethsemane and Mary Magdalene's penitence, along with Augustine's *Confessions*. One day, while gazing at a portrait of Christ, she was deeply moved by the wounds covering His body. Weeping profusely, she cast herself down before the painting, and solemnly pleaded for the Lord to sustain and strengthen her.

At that moment, Teresa discerned that she was delivered of her worldly interests, and from that time forward, as best she could, sought to make Christ's sufferings the center of her prayers and His service her single goal.

Daybreak

But small is the gate and narrow the road that leads to life, and only a few find it. Matthew 7:14

Though Teresa was convinced these graces came from God, she was well aware that others had been duped by the Devil through their imagination, and she actively searched out counsel from numerous church officials to confirm the source of her inspiration.

Some of these advisors were supportive; others persecuted her severely. Of particular benefit was a Jesuit priest, Father Balthasar Alvarez, who recommended that Teresa would do well to ask God to do what was most pleasing to Him and to recite a hymn, called the "Veni Creator Spiritus," every day. Once, while saying the appointed lyrics, she was filled with ecstatic rapture and heard God say inside her soul: "I will have thee converse now, not with men, but with angels" — an especially significant insight, considering Teresa's conversational talents and sensitivity to others' opinions!

"True humility is not an abject, groveling, self-despising spirit; it is but a right estimate of ourselves as God sees us," Tryon Edwards asserted.[13] There are no better words to describe Teresa's humble-but-not-servile demeanor in the years following this life-changing revelation.

For a time, Teresa frequently experienced these interior speeches, explaining that she could hear the words more clearly and distinctly than if she had been listening with her ears. She also pointed out that, as a result of these visions, virtuous impressions were made on her soul, overwhelming her with God's assurance of their accuracy and bestowing joy and peace upon her — the Holy Spirit's unmistakable fruit.

Perhaps even more important, it was during this time that Teresa began to see Jesus as her closest companion with whom she could speak directly and openly, saying:

> I saw that, although God, He was also Man, and is not dismayed at the weaknesses of men, for He understands our miserable nature, liable as it is to frequent falls, because of man's first sin for which He had come to make reparation. Although He is my Lord, I can talk to Him as a friend, because He is not, I believe, like those whom we call lords on earth.... O King of glory and Lord of all kinds! Thy kingdom is not fenced in by trifles, but is infinite. No third party is required to obtain an audience of Thee. We have only to look at Thy person to see at once that Thou alone deservest to be called Lord.[14]

Facing Difficulties

Blessed are you when people insult you, persecute you and falsely say all kinds of evil against you because of me. Matthew 5:11–12

For three years, Teresa endured rigid opposition. In 1557, when Peter of Alcantara (who, like Teresa, was canonized later also) visited Avila and met with the much-persecuted nun, he proclaimed that nothing was more plainly evident to him than God's conduct of her soul.

Reassured by Peter's counsel, Teresa considered how best to serve Christ, and as she prayerfully reflected on her Order's too-lax lifestyle, commended the matter to God.

When her niece, also a resident at the Carmelite convent, raised the possibility of starting a smaller, enclosed community, Teresa believed the idea to be divinely inspired. After enlisting the financial and spiritual aid of an impressive retinue of benefactors — including Dona Guiomar de Ulloa, a wealthy widow, Peter of Alcantara, Louis Bertrand, and the Bishop of Avila — Teresa obtained the necessary papers to begin the new work from Father Gregory Fernandez, the Carmelites' prior provincial. But as soon as the project was formally approved, fiery opposition fell upon Teresa and her supporters — particularly upon Father Gregory, whose own license was revoked.

But the Lord did not abandon Teresa to her opponents. With the encouragement of a Dominican monk, Father Ibanez, and Dona Guiomar's financial assistance, Teresa refused to retreat. Sustained by God's grace and her belief in the need for change, her remarkable reform of the Carmelite Order was launched in complete secrecy and, after twenty-five years as a nun, she started with a new identity for herself.

Having kept her mother's name earlier — Teresa de Ahumada — now, she asked to be known simply as Teresa of Jesus.

In 1561, her sister, Dona Juana, started with her husband to construct a convent while giving observers the impression that the house would be a dwelling for her family. The intentionally spartan design of the Order's house, small and poor as it was, nonetheless ensured that its inhabitants, needs would be met. It was here that Teresa spent her happiest five years.

When a document authorizing the establishment of the new convent arrived from Rome the next year, excitement broke out as Teresa's relieved supporters witnessed the timely opening of the new convent, but many townspeople, watching Dona Juana's just-built house turn into a nunnery almost overnight, were suddenly stunned. Viewing Teresa's stringent reforms as a criticism of the local Catholic establishment and afraid that the unendowed convent would become an economic burden to the city, many of Avila's citizens continued to wreak havoc. At one point, Sega, the papal nuncio, denounced Teresa as "a restless gadabout, disobedient, contumacious woman who promulgates pernicious doctrine under pretense of devotion."

To answer the rising protests, the mayor and the magistrate conspired to demolish the building in an attempt to close the convent down, but at the last minute, another providentially placed Dominican friend, Father Banez, managed to talk them out of it. In the course of time, Teresa aided in the establishment of thirty more monasteries and convents.

Meanwhile, as the slanders, insults, and accusations rained down upon her, the inspired innovator found her steady source of comfort in God. "With so good a Friend and Captain ever present, Himself the first to suffer, everything can be borne," Teresa avows in her *Life*. "He helps. He strengthens. He never fails. He is the true Friend."[15] Facing the onslaught with gracious equanimity and patient persistence, she continued to pray and remained at peace in the eye of the storm.

The Reluctant Witness

For everyone who asks receives; he who seeks finds; and to him who knocks, the door will be opened. Matthew 7:8

*I*t is not as if Teresa welcomed all the attention. She herself prayed to be delivered from the raptures she received from God. Believing that women were more vulnerable to visionary experiences than men, she cautioned others not to seek this gift, lest they succumb to "spiritual gluttony."

Unlike many medieval saints, Teresa did not think that spiritual ecstasy is equal to holiness. Stressing the necessity of loving Christ through service to humanity, she warned, "Let everyone understand that real love of God does not consist in tear-shedding, nor in that sweetness and tenderness for which we usually long, just because they console us, but in serving God in justice, fortitude of soul, and humility."[16]

Teresa's common sense, disciplined outlook, and trust in God's provision, combined with her talents of brilliant administration and an extraordinary capacity for hard work, enabled her to overcome obstacles that less-gifted people would find impossible to surmount. "As a child Teresa had been moved by hopes of Heaven; as an adolescent she was swayed by thoughts and fears of Hell," writes biographer Allison Peers in *Mother of Carmel*. "Yet in her mature life [many years later], she was to be surpassed by none for her complete selflessness."[17]

Emphasizing the benefits of a small-sized religious community, Teresa founded her first cloister, St. Joseph of Avila, with thirteen nuns. In choosing candidates for the community, perceptive

insight and good judgment were among Teresa's top criteria —
"God preserve us from stupid nuns!" she insisted, believing that
smart people see their faults and are open to guidance — and
showed the sisters what she expected by example, taking her turn
at sweeping floors, spinning wool, and washing dishes. Manual
work and alms, rather than impressive dowries and celebrated
patrons' donations, provided the means to support this simple
lifestyle.

To signify their personal identification with Jesus' poverty,
the Carmelite nuns wore coarse, brown, monklike habits and
sparse sandals made of rope, earning them the title "discalced," or
barefoot. They cropped their hair, slept on straw, abstained from
eating meat, and kept silence during meals. Members strictly
remained within the enclosed convent. Not an easy way of life at
any time in history but an understandable Christian response,
given Teresa's cultural context as a Spanish Catholic woman with
an aristocratic background (her seven brothers all became con-
quistadors) living during a perniciously tumultuous era.

By 1567, when the prior general of the Carmelites, Father
Rubeo, visited Teresa at St. Joseph's, he was so impressed with
the results of her reforms that he granted her permission to found
more of the controversial communities, including two houses for
friars, known as the "Contemplative Carmelites," whose oversight
Teresa passed to John-of-the-Cross in 1570.

One by one, additional convents and monasteries opened.
Against incredible odds, the visionary leader indomitably forged
ahead, facing rugged mountain ranges, rough weather, militant
opponents, and deteriorating health on her way to establishing
sixteen houses in less than twenty years.

The Language of Surrender

*When you pray, go into your room, close the door and
pray to your Father, who is unseen. Then your Father,
who sees what is done in secret, will reward you.* Matthew 6:6

When she was sixty-two, Teresa's physician informed her
during an exam that he could find no single infirmity to
center his attention on — too many ailments, including rheumatoid

arthritis, chronic digestive problems, and cardiovascular disease, gripped her long-afflicted body. Seeming to be only half-conscious of her body's tenuous condition, she continued toting the well-worn tent on numerous treks across Spain and, on at least one occasion, when her beloved younger brother Lorenzo perished in America, wondered why "I never quite manage to die." She suffered, then survived, two heart attacks and, at the end, developed throat cancer before going to be with God in 1582. In spite of her ever-increasing physical debilitation, it was during these last years that Teresa's ministry truly blossomed.

Under orders to explain exactly what her spiritual practices and experiences were, Teresa was forced to write down her life story. There can be no doubt from the sheer transparency of her self-examination that she never guessed that these explicit pages would be published later, let alone be distributed across the world.

A vibrant testimony to the wonders of the Holy Spirit at work in a woman with a wide-open heart toward God, her refreshingly genuine *Life* turned out to be nothing less than an unabashed declaration of love. Its literary power undiminished after four centuries, Teresa's autobiography provides an almost shocking glimpse into the saint's mind and soul, giving us a palpable taste for what it must have been like for her to grow up hungry for God and, finally, to find true satisfaction at the age of fifty-seven.

By inviting us to plunge with her into the depths of her fervent devotion, Teresa aims us toward heaven's heights. Not for the fainthearted (or the closed-minded), the detailed account outdazzles most current Christian novels in its dynamic display of disorienting spiritual somersaults and whizbang special effects.

The strange thing is, Teresa's tale is real.

But she did not stop there. *The Way of Perfection*, her second book, was written to supply much-needed advice to her nuns about quiet prayer. Both playful and practical, it was intended to be used as a warm "family" guide among Teresa's cloistered sisters only, and as such, her humorously self-deprecating remarks, thinly veiled references to church critics ("If anyone should tell you that prayer is dangerous, consider him the real danger and run from him"), and abundant practical hints are dished out, undiluted, for her seasoned disciples' benefit. Love, however, is the book's dominant flavor, with plenty of sweetly spiritual imagery sprinkled in for good measure.

Interior Castle, Teresa's formal treatise on prayer, remains an outstanding classic. Aimed at a broader audience than her earlier works, its language of surrender poignantly portrays the exclusive nature of Teresa's private union with Christ in prayer. Believing that not everyone would encounter what she did, her emphasis lies rather in promoting each individual's intimacy with Jesus, not whether every Christian should try to repeat her personal experiences.

Throughout all of her books, Teresa is as blunt about discussing her foibles and faults as she is in describing her colorful visions. Her struggle is, after all, a familiar one. Is there any believer who, desiring to know Christ more deeply, is not continually thwarted by countless distractions?

Common Ground

Let your light shine before men, that they may see your good deeds and praise your Father in heaven. Matthew 5:16

O that we of the twentieth century in affluent ambiances were as sensitive to the traps and snares of materialism and the need to affirm constantly the presence of the Lord in our devotion to Him!" succinctly observes Dr. Clayton L. Berg, Jr., president of the Latin American Mission, reflecting on the lasting impact of Teresa's persuasive story. "I am convinced that the major obstacle to that wholeness and completeness in my life is that to which she so eloquently confesses on several occasions — the hard work that is required to detach ourselves from ourselves through the practice of virtues and fidelity to prayer."[18]

Teresa's detachment from the world mirrors Mary of Bethany's devotion to Christ; for the saintly Carmelite reformer, loving Jesus was her premier life focus.

Her passionate witness, still remarkably relevant, resonates sweetly and clearly. Smiling, we are drawn closer to God's throne, hearing Teresa's heart echoing through the words she left behind.

Listen: "We must begin prayer by feeling no doubt that unless we allow ourselves to be defeated we are sure to succeed. This is certain, for however insignificant our conquest may be, we shall come off with great gains.

"Never fear that the Lord who invites us to drink of the fountain will allow us to die of thirst."[19] Here is a sacrificial saint we can relate to — if we are willing to receive the best of what her wise words offer.

Naturally, we will view Teresa through the lens of our own doctrines and traditions as we sort through each text, but this need not pose a lasting barrier to receiving from her what is most relevant to us. "Across the difference of four centuries and the prejudices of religious differences, Teresa reaches out to us all," Oxford University's Dr. James L. Houston points out. "She fills us with the breath of prayer, and she challenges us to enrich our interior lives more fully with the presence of Christ.

"My mother, a Protestant missionary to Spain, was stoned out of a village near Avila, the place where Teresa lived. With that experience as a child, I never thought that I would come to admire the devotion of this Catholic woman," admits Dr. Houston honestly. "Yet the more I have tried to understand the spirit of Teresa, the more I feel the depth of her fervor to God, in her desire to be like Christ and in her practical realism as the founder of seventeen convents."[20]

Listen . . .

> Let nothing disturb you.
> Let nothing terrify you.
> All things pass away.
> God is unchangeable.
> Patience gains everything.
> He who clings to God wants nothing.
> God alone is sufficient.
>
> — Teresa of Jesus, *Maxims*

∴ 🍇 ∵

Jesus! The very thought of Thee
With sweetness fills my breast;
But sweeter far Thy face to see,
And in Thy presence rest.
No voice can sing, no heart can frame
Nor can the mem'ry find
A sweeter sound than Thy blest name,
O Savior of mankind!
O hope of ev'ry contrite heart!
O Joy of all the Meek!
To those who ask, how kind Thou art!
How good to those who seek!
But what to those who find? Ah! This
No tongue nor pen can show;
The love of Jesus, what it is,
None but His loved ones know.
Jesus, our only joy be Thou,
As Thou our prize wilt be;
In Thee be all our glory now,
And through eternity.

— Bernard of Clairvaux (1091–1153)

CONCLUSION

*W*hile standing in the shower, it struck me: However much I long to spend time alone with Jesus, as Mary and Teresa did, my life is filled with constant interruptions. I do not live in a cloistered convent; I live in a hectic household.

My various private roles — wife, mother, grandmother, daughter, sister, and friend — must also blend with varied public guises as I move about in a sphere of ministry that often does not clearly distinguish between what is "sacred" and "secular." For me, the question is not whether to sacrificially devote my attention Christ, but how.

If I "detach" in order to exclusively enjoy my Beloved's presence, I must also be able to "reattach" right away, when necessary. An impending appointment or a knock at my door can bring an abrupt end to silent fellowship with the Savior. I long for more.

Then I realized: All saints face this same challenge. It was not as if Mary lived in some steady state of ethereal bliss, away from the pressures and problems of "the world." She could see and touch Jesus, but she could also be seen and be touched, and Mary's emotions registered her critic's reactions.

How did she find the balance? She could not spend time waiting endlessly at Jesus' feet. Other things called out for her attention too. How did Mary know which, and when, to choose?

Think about Teresa. She invested her entire lifetime in learning how to sacrificially love and serve the Lord. She did not have an overworked husband to go bed with, or an eight-hour job to report to, or a teetering toddler to protect. The constant demands and distractions of common contemporary life — noisy traffic, beauty pressures, media intrusions, and the regular ringing of the telephone — did not disrupt her days.

Yet, unlike John the Baptist, Teresa did not reside in the desert as a locust-eating hermit, either. Somehow, she discovered how to spend one-on-one time "alone" with Jesus in the midst of her real-life religious community (no wonder Teresa reduced the size of her convent from 140 to 13 women and instituted strict rules of silence!), extensive travels, and hard work. She found a way to ease everyday transitions between solitude and society.

Like Mary, who chose the better way by making it a priority to sit at Jesus' feet and taking time out to listen to Him, we, too, will find that His loving approval welcomes those who highly value the blessing of His presence. Like Teresa, we can offer ourselves as living sacrifices to the Lord, stubbornly refusing to let the world press us into its powerful, pre-set patterns, as we are being transformed by the renewing of our minds.

For their devotion, these saints found inexpressible joy in Jesus' presence — a priceless treasure available to all who worship the Lord in singleness of heart. What greater reward than this can we possibly hope for?

We have much to learn from these women's stories. But, if we compare ourselves too closely to them, we may miss something important: the unique gifts and ministry God gives to each one of us to express for His glory; the one-of-a-kind life pattern He delightfully creates and designs for every Christian to grow into.

"Sameness is to be found among the most 'natural' men," admonishes C. S. Lewis in *Mere Christianity*, "not among those who surrender to Christ. How monotonously alike all the great tyrants and conquerors have been; how gloriously different are the saints.

"But," he adds, "there must be a real giving up of the self.... Your real new self (which is Christ's and also yours, and yours because it is His) will not come as long as you are looking for it. It will come when you are looking for Him.... Look for yourself, and you will find in the long run only hatred, loneliness, despair, rage, ruin, and decay. But look for Christ and you will find Him, and with Him, everything else thrown in."[21]

Mary and Teresa knew this secret. For one, an alabaster box containing costly ointment represented the worshipful outpouring of her life at Jesus' feet; for the other, the slow-building momentum of sacrificial devotion to Christ over more than half a century remains her lasting legacy to the power of God's triumphant love. Each "did what she could do." And it is the same for each of us.

Points of Reflection

1. Living to please others interferes with living to please the Lord when . . .
2. I believe that the grace of devotion is sometimes confused with . . .
3. When I think about Mary of Bethany's anointing Jesus, I realize that the greatest obstacle to sacrificial love for Christ in my life is . . .
4. Jesus' statement to Martha, "Mary has chosen what is better," reminds me that . . .
5. In Teresa of Avila's story, I found it encouraging to see . . .
6. My most memorable encounter with joy in Jesus' presence was . . .

Prayer: Jesus, enlarge my capacity to love You. Grant me the grace of devotion that I may enjoy wholehearted communion with You. Strengthen me by Your Spirit, Lord: revive my desire to spend time alone with You as I sit at Your feet. In Your name, I pray. Amen.

~: 🍇 :~

How lovely is your dwelling place,
O LORD Almighty!
My soul yearns, even faints,
for the courts of the LORD;
my heart and my flesh cry out
for the living God.
Even the sparrow has found a home,
and the swallow a nest for herself,
where she may have her young —
a place near your altar.
O LORD Almighty, my King and my God.
Blessed are those who dwell in your house;
they are ever praising you.
Blessed are those whose strength is in you;
who have set their hearts on pilgrimage.

— Psalm 84:1–5

The secret heart is devotion's temple;
there the saint lights the flame of purest sacrifice,
which burns unseen but not unaccepted.[22]

— Hannah More (1745–1833)

Chapter Six

It is not the possession of extraordinary gifts that
makes extraordinary usefulness, but the dedication of
what we have to the service of God.[1]
— Frederick William Robertson ((1816–1853)

*Y*ou did not choose me: I chose you" (John 15:16 NEB). Chosen to go and bear fruit, said Jesus — fruit that will last.
Precisely chosen, moved into ministry by our Father's hand. To
nourish and comfort in some way the souls God loves, summoned
as His servants.

But there are times when the grace of service is quite different
from what we had in mind.

More than a few of my friends have been surprised by the
Holy Spirit's perfectly timed nudges over the years. Take Rachel,
for example. Previously a stay-at-home mom with two preschool
sons, my former prayer partner sensed God's irresistible tug
toward missions ministry. So, along with her husband, Jim, a college instructor, she started looking into overseas service opportu-
nities. Seven years went by. Rachel and Jim completed special-
ized bachelor's degrees; summer sessions supplemented their
missions training; their prayer life deepened.

Within a few more years, Rachel and Jim hope to be "in the
field," complementing each other's vocations as workers with
Wycliffe Bible Translators.

"We're open to what the Lord would have us do," says Rachel,
"though it's not always as simple as it sounds. Many things had to
fit together for us to get this far in the missions preparation
process, and there are still many steps left for us to take."

In spite of the uncertainties related to her calling, Rachel has found a place of acceptance with her current circumstances. "Being open to God's direction has boiled down to being willing to be quiet as we wait — which, at times, is unbelievably hard to do," she admits. "It also amounts to accepting the fact that we may not go, if that is what the Lord wants in the long run. In the meantime, our 'normal' day-to-day life continues to keep me busy: church ministry, the boys' football games, nursing home visits with Jim's grandmother, and managing our household on a tight budget.

"Though sometimes it seems like we're never going to get there, I'm confident that we're heading in the right direction," shares my friend.

By asking, "Lord, what work would You have me be doing?" Rachel sees every day as an opportunity to love, serve, and enjoy God. It is not always easy, but she knows she does not have to put off using her talents and energy as Christ's disciple until some future date.

Kim's Christian calling was also a challenge, but for different reasons. She and her husband, Denny, had met in Bible college, married the summer after graduation, and moved to a medium-size town in the North, where Denny was hired to work as an assistant pastor at a rapidly growing church. After their arrival, Kim continued her schooling at a nearby university while working part time as a teacher.

When I became better acquainted with Kim, she shared with me about how pressured she felt regarding other people's expectations of what she should be doing as a pastor's wife — an irritating fact of life that college had not prepared her for. At school, she had been encouraged to use her gifts, fine-tune her skills, think things through, and continually pray for vocational discernment. But in "the real world," she discovered that her motives were frequently questioned. A small handful of church members expected her to be as involved in church activities as Denny was. Undaunted by others' criticism, and with her husband's encouragement she continued to follow the Lord's leading.

"Denny is, and has always been, 110 percent supportive of what I'm doing," Kim told me. "We see a tremendous need in the church for qualified women counselors, and I can't shake off the burden that God's placed on my heart in this regard. But it's obvious I can't do everything at once. If I'm a full-time student, working toward co-ministry with Denny, the amount of church work I can do right now is relatively limited."

Over several years, Kim and Denny obtained their graduate degrees; their joint calling eventually led them to open a counseling service together. Staying on a steady course in the same direction, they remain convinced that the Holy Spirit has directed them into a specific area of ministry, demonstrating by their daily witness that lifelong Christian vocation comes in many forms.

Countless striking examples, with each life pattern so uniquely varied from the next, are potent reminders that every one of us been chosen and called for a divine purpose — stories about women like Bev, a gifted watercolor artist, believed to be cured of Hodgkin's disease, stepping out in faith with her husband, Randy, to adopt their infant son; Carol, an incest victim who recently earned her social work degree and now plans to establish an outreach to other sexually abused women; Anne, a pastor's wife who creatively blends her supporting role at church with several others — home-schooling mom, childbirth educator, hostess, cook, and wise advisor; Sally, a registered oncology nurse and co-pastor of a college campus ministry; and Andrea, a syndicated talk-show host and mother of five, hired to conduct phone interviews via Moody Broadcasting Company's studio linkup in her home. These courageous Christians, called by the King and commissioned for His service, are fulfilling their vocations as they quietly heed and respond to their Savior's summons. And they are not alone: Every follower of Jesus has a key part to play in serving Christ's kingdom.

Each one of us has a position to fill and a job to do. As born-again employees with a brand-new Boss, Jesus matches us with a specific task and makes us fruitful according to His promise.

Our given status or ranking is not the main issue. (Unless, of course, one considers what Jesus said about the valued privilege of His kingdom's best position — the "last place.") All we do is simply ask for the grace to say, "Send me, Lord," without any qualifiers, and be willing to do whatever job is required of us. Then, somewhere along the way, the call comes. We do not do the choosing; God does.

To serve in a position of ministry, Dr. Roberta Hestenes, president of Eastern College in St. David's, Pennsylvania, recommends that a woman "should become a person of prayer and spiritual discernment, so that she really is seeking to minister out of her desire to be Christ's person and obedient to the will of God." Furthermore, Dr. Hestenes adds, "She should be willing to take risks, including the risk of not being approved of by everybody."

Serving the Lord is a grace that we can receive with dignity and joy. As believers belonging to the church today, we can follow the examples of women in the Word who shared their gifts and resources with Jesus. And what an incredible history we have to encourage us — almost two thousand years' worth of written testimonies and the saints' witness across time, urging us by their words and deeds to worship the great Lamb upon His throne.

Consider our first role models who helped to establish the early church: Lydia, a "dealer in purple cloth," whose home became a meeting place for the apostles; Phoebe, commended by Paul in a special citation as "servant of the church in Cenchrea"; Mary, Tryphena, Tryphosa, and Persis — all highlighted for working "very hard in the Lord." And Priscilla, Aquila's wife and Apollos' teacher, the tentmaker Paul affectionately called "my fellow worker." Like them, our usefulness to God does not depend on achieving a sinless state but on letting go of our old notions about status and self-importance; like them, we are gifted to serve in God's kingdom.

But before these saints were born, there was another woman the Lord called upon to fulfill a special task whose witness shines brightly across the centuries, illuminating our Christian commission today. Jewish by marriage, she was an outcast and an alien, a stranger living in a strange land. But an inspired pledge of service made alongside a dusty road brought her lasting honor.

Her name was Ruth.

Ruth's Story

~: 🍇 :~

*T*he Book of Ruth's opening scene is sadly tragic: Three stranded widows with no male heirs are separated from their kin and property, cut off from a hoped-for inheritance by the death of their husbands.

Naomi, a Hebrew wife and mother from famine-ravaged Bethlehem, has been away from home for at least a decade, maybe much longer. At the time of her arrival in Moab, Judah's border country across the Jordan River, Naomi had a spouse named Elimelech and two sons, Mahlon and Kilion. Elimelech died first. The boys married a couple of local girls, Orpah and Ruth, and settled down.

A mother could not have asked for a better set of daughters. Things were looking up. Then the sons died, both of them — just like that — leaving Naomi with only two young Moabite widows and no visible means of support.

Upon hearing that the Lord is aiding Israel through blessing the season's grain harvest, Naomi considers her options. It does not take long before she realizes what she must do.

After making preparations to return to Bethlehem, the three women pack up their things and set out on the road toward Judah. Suddenly, reality hits. "Go back, each of you, to your mother's home," cries Naomi with convincing conviction, stopping to face squarely her two daughters-in-law. Perhaps she is also silently thinking: *Surely my son's wives, who are both Moabites, will see the wisdom in immediately returning to their birthplace.*

"May the LORD show kindness to you, as you have shown to your dead and to me," continues Naomi persuasively. "May the LORD grant that each of you will find rest in the home of another husband" (Ruth 1:8–9). Then, momentarily stanching her tears, she leans over and kisses both of them after extending the double maternal blessing.

Weeping loudly, Orpah and Ruth protest Naomi's request. They will not hear of parting from their husbands' mother.

Naomi wonders: *Why would these two want to remain with their rapidly aging, opinionated, Jewish mother-in-law when they can go back to their homes instead? I don't have anything left ... nothing. My womb will bear no more sons for my poor girls to marry; and even if, by some miracle of God — blessed be His name — I married today and gave birth to two baby boys, would my daughters wait around long enough to marry them?*

As she voices these purposefully discouraging thoughts, Naomi realizes that, in all likelihood, her Moabite daughters-in-law will not find a warm welcome in Bethlehem.

The Curse That Became a Blessing

> *I am a friend to all who fear you, to all who follow your precepts.* Psalm 119:63

Naomi knows that Israel's relations with Moab are historically hostile, having originated near Sodom and Gomorrah's destruction site. For it was there in a mountain cave not far from the demolished city that Lot's motherless daughters, lacking visible marriage prospects, conceived a wicked plan to produce a couple of family heirs.

Plotting out their pregnancies, they filled their father's wine cup over and over again, then took turns lying down with their dazed and drunken dad. A pair of grandson-sons arrived about forty weeks later — Moab, who eventually established his namesake nation, and Ben Ammi, who later became the father of the Ammonites (Gen. 19:29–38). Both tribes proved to be bitter enemies of Abraham's descendants.

After Israel's exodus from Egypt, Hebrew men engaged in illicit sexual relations and forbidden fertility rites with Moabite women at a place called Baal Peor — a blatant breach of Israel's covenant with God. All offenders were subsequently executed (Num. 25:1–5). Thus, Baal Peor became a long-remembered emblem of Hebrew shame.

While preparing to wage a war of vengeance against the Moab nation for Israel's desecration at Baal Peor, Moses specifically asked if the Moabite women had been allowed to live, explaining: "They were the ones who followed Balaam's advice and were the means of turning the Israelites away from the LORD in what happened at Peor, so that a plague struck the Lord's people" (Num. 31:16). Only virgins were spared in the ensuing slaughter (Num. 31:18 and 35).

When Moses died, he was buried in Moab (Deut. 34:5). Shortly before his death, Israel's greatest prophet issued this solemn edict: "No Ammonite or Moabite or any of his descendants may enter the assembly of the LORD, even down to the tenth generation. For they did not come to meet you with bread and water on your way when you came out of Egypt, and they hired Balaam ... to pronounce a curse on you. However, the LORD your God would not listen to Balaam but turned the curse into a blessing for you, because the LORD your God loves you. Do not seek a treaty of friendship with them as long as you live" (Deut. 23:3–6).

Naomi's familiarity with Jewish history informs her that Judah is likely to be a harsh, hazardous place for Ruth and Orpah; she has no choice but to vehemently discourage her daughters-in-law from joining her on the long, 120-mile journey home. She will miss them — much more than either of the women apparently realizes — but she loves her son's widows too much to ask them to suffer possible bias, bigotry, and banishment for her sake. So, Naomi bravely tries one last time to turn them back toward Moab.

"Return home, my daughters," implores their desolate mother-in-law. "Why would you come with me?" (Ruth 1:11).

What Naomi does not know is that Ruth will not be leaving.

Ruth's Reply

Direct me in the path of your commands,
for there I find delight. Psalm 119:35

Mahlon's widow, who is quite familiar with her mother-in-law's methods of persuasion, patiently listens to Naomi's repetitious pleas. Over the years, she has grown to appreciate this stalwart matriarch's buoyant outlook. Storm survival is nothing new to Naomi. She is anchored to the one true God of Israel. Who can shake her?

Ruth does not even attempt to argue with the wailing widow. She stands by, waiting for the right moment to vow her allegiance, impressed by Naomi's creative tactics. But Ruth is not moved. Years of residing with this resilient Hebrew woman has profoundly influenced Ruth, providing her with a new identity that cannot be instantly discarded at will along an arid road east of town.

Ruth has learned to ride out the rough weather too.

The mother-in-law's irrepressible pleas raze Orpah's resistance, however. In tears, she chooses to comply with the good woman's commands, quickly kisses her good-bye, and then vanishes from Naomi's life. But Ruth will not be moved. She clings to her maternal mentor, fervently gripping the sweet-smelling garments as her teardrops touch the dust.

Naomi makes one last bid for her devoted daughter-in-law's freedom. "Look," she says sharply, motioning in Orpah's direction, "your sister-in-law is going back to her people and her gods. Go back with her" (Ruth 1:15).

Return to Chemosh, the worthless idol Naomi hates? To Moab, where regularly scheduled human sacrifices fail to satiate the demon's hunger? Back to the place where Mahlon is buried and family ties remain permanently changed by the strain of an interfaith alliance? Away from the lasting comfort of a mother who speaks of the living God with steadfast loyalty and tender conviction? Never.

"Don't urge me to leave you or to turn back from you. Where you go I will go, where you stay I will stay. Your people will be my people and your God my God. Where you die I will die, and there I will be buried.

"May the LORD deal with me, be it ever so severely, if anything but death separates you and me" (Ruth 1:16–17).

The sorrowful scene shifts. Naomi notices that Ruth's wet face has a radiant glow. For once in her life, Elimelech's widow is at a loss for words.

Return to Judah

My comfort in my suffering is this: Your promise preserves my life. Psalm 119:50

$\mathcal{T}$raveling alone on the open road, the two women resume their tiring trek to Bethlehem. With barely enough money to get by on and no future means of support expected, Ruth and Naomi's social isolation intensifies, strengthening their mutual bond as they negotiate a dangerous route that carries them over the rough terrain.

Droughty steppeland roads, brisk mountain ascents, long stretches through stifling valleys, and two major waterways — the Arnon and Jordan Rivers — pose a significant threat to the widows' safety and stamina. Much of the scenery is unfamiliar to Ruth, who secretly doubts that her mother-in-law would have been able to find safe passage along this winding, unprotected path if she had insisted on going ahead by herself.

Cutting through Moab-Judah border territory was a high-risk venture for anyone in those days, given the nations' simmering suspicions and ongoing conflicts. But for two women on a trip without watchguards? It had to be the result of sheer lunacy. Or, as it happened to be in this particular case, a clear act of faith.

Understandably, when the worn-out women finally reach Bethlehem sans husbands, the whole town starts to stir. "Can this be Naomi?" the women exclaim (Ruth 1:19). Facing her friends for the first time in more than a decade, Naomi, formerly Elimelech's wife and the mother of Mahlon and Kilion, tells them to call her by a new name.

"Call me Mara," she says, because her birth name, which means "pleasant," no longer fits; "bitter" now becomes her better. "I went away full, but the LORD has brought me back empty," observes the forlorn, fatigued widow. "Why call me Naomi?" (Ruth 1:212).

Ruth, the Moabitess, is standing near her mother-in-law as the mournful words continue to pour forth. Looking around in search of a friendly smile, the young widow sees only strangers' stares — the rude faces of Ephrathite women who have been conditioned by long-standing enmities to despise and mistrust Ruth's tribe. Naomi's neighbors cannot quite manage to extend their sympathy to a much-hated Moabite.

Mahlon's bereaved wife has just traveled for 120 perilous miles. The woman that she accompanied on the exhausting excursion seems to be capable of thinking only of herself. Her story makes it sound as if Ruth has played no part in promoting Naomi's survival over these past weeks. Now, Elimelech's widow wants to be called Mara. Does the presence of her dutiful daughter-in-law even matter to her any longer?

"The LORD has pronounced against me; the Almighty has brought misfortune upon me," groans the senior widow, full of woe (Ruth 1:21 NEB).

Walled in by grief and depression, Naomi apparently does not realize that she is shutting the sensitive girl out at exactly the moment when a gracious introduction might ease Ruth's transition into Bethlehem's tightly knit Jewish community.

"This is how Naomi's daughter-in-law, Ruth the Moabitess, returned with her from Moabite country," the Bible tells us (Ruth 1:22). But as the first chapter of Ruth's story comes to a close, we receive the good news: The barley harvest is beginning in Bethlehem. There will be food and fullness again! Even for empty widows.

In Boaz's Barley Field

*Take away the disgrace I dread,
for your laws are good.* Psalm 119:39

Once again, we are reminded of Ruth's alien status as she seeks Naomi's permission to set out for the barley fields: "And Ruth the Moabitess said to Naomi, 'Let me go to the fields and pick up the leftover grain behind anyone in whose eyes I find favor'" (Ruth 2:2).

Hebrew law allowed for the poor to go gleaning in the reapers' footsteps by following with their baskets behind farmers' harvesters in search of loose grain lying on the ground.

But only a crafty landowner, or a very benevolent one, would be likely to permit a vulnerable woman newly arrived from Jordan's West Bank to gather grain in his field.

Does Ruth realize the danger she is putting herself in? Perhaps. After her long journey to Judah and because of her lonely position as a social outcast, she is learning to depend more deeply on God's love and faithfulness. With no one else offering to provide for them, Ruth willingly takes up the task of gleaning barley, so it is no surprise when God guides her to precisely the perfect place, at exactly the right moment, to the specific spot where she needs to be — an exquisite picture of His providence in action.

Arriving at an unknown farmer's field, Ruth asks permission to start gleaning, and "as it happened, she was in that strip of the fields which belonged to Boaz of Elimelech's family, and there was Boaz coming out from Bethlehem" (Ruth 2:4 NEB). Did Ruth try other farms first? We do not know. All we are told is that as her day's events unfolded, there was Someone much greater than sheer coincidence at work.

Ruth finds more than provision in Boaz's field; she finds peace. After blessing the workers, Boaz makes an inquiry of the harvester's foreman, asking, "Whose young woman is that?" (Ruth 2:5).

Once more, Ruth's ethnic identity leaps into plain view as the servant replies, "She is the Moabitess who came back from Moab with Naomi. She said, 'Please let me glean and gather among the sheaves behind the harvesters.' She went into the field and has worked steadily from morning till now, except for a short rest in the shelter" (Ruth 2:6–7).

Something starts to stir within Boaz. As he listens to the laborer's explanation, the well-established agriculturist sees Naomi's ally gingerly stepping in and out between the barley sheaves. A spring breeze blows softly over the serene landscape. Grassy acres of grain, waving with the sound of rustling silk ribbons, surround Boaz on a momentary isle of calm.

With the April sun's warmth shining down upon his dark skin, the Hebrew landowner looks across the fresh-cut field where Ruth is gleaning barley, still blissfully unaware of Boaz's steady gaze, and finds himself inexplicably drawn to the hard-working widow.

For many moments, he sees no one else.

Tandem Venture

*I am a stranger on earth; do not hide
your commands from me.* Psalm 119:19

*L*ost in concentration and centered on the task at hand, Ruth does not hear Boaz approaching. At the sound of his voice, she turns around, surprised at the sight of Naomi's well-to-do kinsman standing close by. But his words stun her more.

"My daughter, listen to me," he says. And after that, all that Ruth hears amazes her. *He wants me to work in his fields exclusively? He doesn't want me to work anywhere else! I am to stay with his servants, accompanying the women as they go about binding the sheaves — and the men have already been warned not to touch me. And, whenever I thirst, I may simply drink from the water jars now; I don't have to get my own!* (Ruth 2:8–9)

For the first time, Ruth is welcomed with kindness after the long journey from Moab. Her silence has been broken. She is alone in her grief no longer. Setting aside her shock, Ruth bows before her benefactor, exclaiming with astonishment, "Why have I found such favor in your eyes that you notice me — a foreigner?" (Ruth 2:10).

We cannot see Ruth's face: It is lowered to the ground. Is she beautiful? Has something about her physical appearance captured Boaz' fancy?

We are not told what Ruth looked like, although many seem to believe that she was pretty. But what if she is not? Perhaps she is quite plain, with no universally classic allure, lying there in the dust. Since the Bible is curiously silent on this topic (in marked contrast to other Old Testament passages describing women's appearance), let us suppose that there is nothing about this woman, save her spirit's beauty, to draw love from the godly man's heart. How will Boaz respond?

This is his answer: "I've been told all about what you have done for your mother-in-law since the death of your husband — how you left your father and mother and your homeland and came to live with a people you did not know before" (Ruth 2:11).

Clearly, Boaz has been prepared by God for this historic encounter. It is the Lord, not Ruth's looks, who has taught Naomi's kinsman her true value. So he adds, "May the Lord repay you for what you have done. May you be richly rewarded by the Lord, the God of Israel, under whose wings you have come to take refuge" (Ruth 2:11–12).

"May I continue to find favor in your eyes, my lord," Ruth responds. "You have given me comfort and have spoken kindly to your servant — though I do not have the standing of one of your servant girls" (Ruth 2:13).

A few hours later, she finds herself sitting near Boaz, feasting with the other harvesters, as the good man bestows his generosity upon her once again. In just one day, Ruth is rewarded the uncommon honor of belonging to Boaz's blessed team.

A Prudent Plan

You are my refuge and my shield; I have put my hope in your word. Psalm 119:114

Returning home with an unusually large amount of grain, as well as her meal's leftovers, Ruth cannot help but anticipate Naomi's thankful-but-thunderstruck reaction.

"Where did you glean today? Where did you work? Blessed be the man who took notice of you!" (Ruth 2:19). Naomi's tickled amazement uplifts Ruth as she smiles at the sound of Naomi's familiar phrasing. It is just what she thought her mother-in-law would say.

Insisting on a moment-by-moment account of Ruth's first gleaning experience, Naomi is unusually quiet as the young widow offers a detailed description not of her work but of Boaz, "the name of the man I worked with today" (Ruth 2:19). Naomi finds this news immensely satisfying. "The LORD bless him!" she cries, unable to contain her enthusiasm. "He has not stopped showing his kindness to the living and the dead" (Ruth 2:20).

Then Ruth's mother-in-law pauses, and with great meaning behind her carefully chosen words, adds, "That man is our close relative; he is one of our kinsman-redeemers" (Ruth 2:20).

Encouraged by the Lord's direct intervention in her circumstances, Naomi begins to think that there may be a way for Ruth to marry into Elimelech's family, after all. She senses the hand of God at work: The Jewish law of levirate expressly intends for a Hebrew widow with no heir to marry her deceased husband's nearest kinsman and thus to "redeem" the widow's property. But the levirate may also be applied to Ruth — the widow of a Hebrew husband. Though Boaz is not Elimelech's brother, Naomi knows that he may still agree to be her kinsman-redeemer, or *go'el*.

Wisely, she chooses to keep these facts to herself, perhaps thinking, *Is it really true? Might my daughter make a successful match after all? The Lord be praised — with his help, all things are possible! When the time is right, the Lord will provide the words for me to say; for now, it will surely go better with Boaz if Ruth stays discreet. Can a Moabite woman be too careful? Better she should cautiously remain in the background, considering what goes on in our harvest fields.*

No — Ruth must be jealous for her reputation. The special kindness of a local landowner must be viewed only for what it is — Boaz's goodwill toward his widowed neighbors. With the Lord's blessing, there will be no scandal. People in Bethlehem mistrust my Moab-born girl enough as it is. . . . The older widow's thoughts are interrupted by something more — Ruth's revelation that Boaz told her also to stay with his workers until they finished harvesting all of his grain (Ruth 2:21).

Regarding Ruth with gentle concern, Naomi lifts her eyes to meet her daughter-in-law's steady gaze, and says simply, "It will be good for you, my daughter, to go with his girls, because in someone else's field you might be harmed" (Ruth 2:22).

More Wise Words

> *May your unfailing love be my comfort, according to the promise of your servant.* Psalm 119:76

Throughout the remaining harvesttime, Ruth remains close to Boaz's busy women servants all day, maintains her distance from the men, and brings full baskets of gleaned grain to her mother-in-law each night. The weeks pass by uneventfully, with two exceptions: Ruth makes rapid gains in her grasp of Jewish ways, and Boaz's respect for the humble Moabitess deepens.

One day, as the sun-scorched fields surrounding Bethlehem lie silent, Naomi broaches a subject she has been perceptively pondering ever since Ruth's first day on Boaz's farm. "My daughter, I want to see you happily settled," she starts out slowly. "Now there is my kinsman Boaz; you were with his girls" (Ruth 3:1–2 NEB).

If Ruth did not know her mother-in-law so well, she would be totally shocked by what she is hearing. But her reaction is easy to imagine: *Of course I know Boaz! I've seen him from afar, every day, throughout the entire harvest season. What an amazing woman Naomi is—acting as if I don't know whom she's talking about in order to maintain proper traditions, and it's all because she loves me and wants what is best.* Beaming, Ruth eagerly awaits Naomi's next sentence.

"Tonight he will be winnowing barley on the threshing floor. Wash and perfume yourself, put on your best clothes. Then go down to the threshing floor, but do not let him know you are there until he has finished eating and drinking. When he lies down, note the place where he is lying. Then go and uncover his feet and lie down. He will tell you what to do" (Ruth 3:1–4).

Did my mother-in-law just say what I think she said? Can she be serious? For three months, all I've been hearing about is how I must stay away from the men at the compound; today, she's telling me to lie down at Boaz' feet! Obviously, she's been keeping tabs on the two of us all along. It's starting to make sense now. Is this what she has been planning all along?

"I will do whatever you say," Ruth answers (Ruth 3:5), memorizing every detail of Naomi's sage advice. Before long, she finds herself covered in her cloak, standing motionless in the threshing room's shadows. Trying not to make a sound, she patiently awaits Boaz' arrival.

Naomi was right. By the time Boaz comes in from his harvest celebration, he is too happily exhausted following the festivities to notice much of anything going on inside his makeshift sleeping quarters. When Ruth uncovers his feet and lies down near the slumbering fellow, he does not even stir. It is not until midnight that he wakes up, startled out of his dreams, and discovers the fragrant-scented woman lying at his feet.

Meeting at Midnight

I have sought your face with all my heart; be gracious to me according to your promise. Psalm 119:58

Naturally, Boaz wants to know immediately who the bold intruder is. "I am your servant, Ruth," is her unruffled reply. "Now spread your skirt over your servant, because you are my next-of-kin" (Ruth 3:9 NEB).

This seems to be precisely what her peaceable protector has been waiting to hear. "The LORD bless you, my daughter," he says somewhat groggily, shaking off the effects of sleep and wine. "This kindness is greater than that which you showed earlier: You have not run after the younger men, whether rich or poor" (Ruth 3:10). For reasons that Ruth cannot fully comprehend, Boaz has not slammed the door on her daring design; he is opening his heart to her instead.

"Set your mind at rest, my daughter," she hears him whisper. "I will do whatever you ask; for, as the whole neighborhood knows, you are a capable woman" (Ruth 3:11 NEB).

With this soothing affirmation, Boaz submits himself to Ruth's legal claim. But that is not all. Naomi's kinsman is also willing to act on Ruth's behalf if anyone disputes the matter. There is another potential *go'el* of closer relation who may wish to wed Mahlon's widow, and by doing so, acquire Mahlon's land; Boaz promises to meet with him in the morning. If the man in question waives this right, Boaz vows before God that he will redeem Ruth, swearing: "I will do it" (Ruth 3:13). Then he tells her to lie quietly until morning.

Getting up before anyone can see who she is, Ruth rises in the morning darkness and prepares to leave. Boaz reminds her not to let anyone know of her visit and asks Ruth to hold out her shawl. Scooping up six full measures of barley, he pours the precious food into the fabric's expanding folds, then lightly places the well-worn garment over her shoulders. Dawn is beginning to break on Bethlehem's hilly horizon.

On her way out the door, Ruth wraps the weighted, hand-loomed cloak around her body; the heavy grain reminds her of carrying a baby yet to be born. In spite of the cool night air, she is warmed by this thought and by Boaz' tender promise as she walks swiftly back to town.

"How did it go?" Naomi inquires as soon as her daughter-in-law steps inside the house, noticing that Ruth's cheeks are far more flushed than usual (Ruth 3:16). Listening intently to every detail, Naomi manages to contain her joy for a little longer, though she feels almost certain of what tomorrow will bring.

"Wait, my daughter, until you find out what happens," she says sensibly. "For the man will not rest until the matter is settled today" (Ruth 3:18).

Redeeming the Family Line

*Remember your word to your servant, for you
have given me hope.* Psalm 119:49

The story ends happily. Boaz, who is a brilliant negotiator in addition to being a productive farmer, meets with ten of the town's elders at the city gate later that same day. By careful maneuvering, he persuasively convinces Elimelech's relative that purchasing Naomi's land might be a poor choice in the long run: Any children born to Ruth would hold inheritance rights also and thus jeopardize the man's entire estate. "You redeem it yourself," the relative tells Boaz. "I cannot do it" (Ruth 4:6). Then, to formally legalize the property transfer, the *go'el* who has just forfeited his right to Elimelech's inheritance removes his shoe — Israel's official sign of a sealed contract in those days.

Standing before the attentive assembly, Boaz makes the extraordinary wedding announcement: "You are witnesses today that I have acquired from Naomi all that belonged to Elimelech and all that belonged to Mahlon and Chilion; and, further, that I have myself acquired Ruth the Moabitess, wife of Mahlon, to be my wife, to perpetuate the name of the deceased with his patrimony, so that his name may not be missing among his kindred and at the gate of his native place. You are witnesses this day" (Ruth 4:9–10 NEB).

This is how Boaz, the son of Rahab, Jericho's redeemed prostitute, and Ruth, Mahlon's widow and a member of the despised Moab nation — the great-grandparents of King David and Jesus' elder ancestors — were joined together by God's divine plan.

Amanda's Story

~: 🍇 :~

"*H*e that sees the beauty of holiness, or true moral good, sees the greatest and most important thing in the world," wrote Jonathan Edwards in his "Treatise of Religious Affections." "Unless this is seen, nothing is seen that is worth seeing: For there is no other true excellence or beauty."[2]

To Amanda Berry Smith, the beauty of holiness was not available only to Bible characters, famous saints, and cloistered clergypersons: She believed that the benefits of sanctification were to be enjoyed by every believer. Her remarkable life, filled with hard work and constant hope, is a brilliant testimony to women of all ages — the lasting example of a simple scrubwoman transformed by God's grace.

Born into slavery in Long Green, Maryland, in 1837, Amanda's faith was nurtured best by Mariam Mathews, her mother, and her grandmother. Both were ardent Christians. Amanda's father, Samuel Berry, also proved to be a powerful example. She describes him as "a strong man, with an excellent constitution, [whom] God wonderfully helped"[3] in his struggle for liberty. Making corn brooms and husk mats every day for his master, Samuel yearned to purchase his freedom, and when harvesttime came, he would walk four miles at the end of the day to work in the fields until one or two o'clock in the morning, return home to sleep for an hour or two, then wake up in the morning and start all over again.

Years later, Amanda's attitude toward work and ministry, which was no doubt shaped in part by her father's experience, exhibited the same dauntless determination.

In *An Autobiography: The Story of the Lord's Dealings with Amanda Smith*, Amanda recalls her mother and grandmother praying for the salvation of Mariam's mistress, Miss Celie; when the happy event finally took place at a Methodist camp meeting, they all rejoiced with tears. But when the young woman's parents found out about it, they forbade her to attend church with the two slaves and separated her from Amanda's mother. Even so, "about a quarter of a mile away was the great dairy," Amanda explains, and "Miss Celie used to slip over there when she got the chance and have a good time praying with mother and grandmother."[4]

Soon after her conversion, Miss Celie contracted typhoid fever. Her last request to her parents before dying was for Mariam and her five children to be liberated from the bondage of slavery. In this way, Amanda Berry became a freewoman at the age of thirteen.

Deep Waters

I call with all my heart; answer me, O LORD,
and I will obey your decrees. Psalm 119:145

United as a family after leaving their separate owners, the Berrys filed their liberation papers in the Baltimore Courthouse and moved to Pennsylvania, where Amanda's eight younger siblings were born in freedom and their home became one of the main stations of the Underground Railroad. There Amanda was hired as a servant for a widowed mother of five children. Especially admired for her southern style of cooking, the hardworking girl soon built a solid reputation with her employer.

Over time, Amanda realized that even though she had attended church meetings since childhood, she had not personally encountered a conversion experience. Trying to be a Christian on her own terms was no longer enough.

Longing to know Christ better, Amanda's prayers were answered at a Baptist revival meeting in 1856. As the only African-American present, the nineteen-year-old housemaid understandably felt timid. Sitting by the back door, she was surprised when a young woman joined her and with tears encouraged the self-conscious visitor to go forward. "She knelt beside me with her arms around me and prayed for me," writes Amanda in her autobiography. "Oh, how she prayed!"[5]

The woman proved to be a powerful witness. By the meeting's end, Amanda stood at the altar and, asking for God's forgiveness, entered into a dramatically changed relationship with Jesus Christ.

Upon arriving at home that night, in the privacy of her room, Amanda resolutely decided that she "would be the Lord's and live for him." Days of prayer, fasting, and continuous Bible study followed. In the years ahead, no cost proved too great for the prayerful disciple who went on to proclaim the kingdom of God in its fullness to thousands of men and women throughout the world.

Amanda's conversion did more than help her cope with the rigors of her daily labor: Her love for Christ also enabled her to endure two difficult marriages and the deaths of four infant children and an adult daughter. Married at the age of seventeen to Calvin M. Devine, she discovered soon afterward that her husband was addicted to alcohol. The brief marriage was filled with strife, and when Calvin was killed in the Civil War, Amanda was forced to work long hours to support herself and her daughter, Mazie.

Her second marriage, to James Smith, a promising preacher associated with the African Methodist Episcopal Church, began with a bitter disappointment. Believing James was about to be appointed a minister through Bethel Church in Philadelphia, Amanda attended a special service and waited to hear her husband's name announced. But James was not on the list. He had decided to leave the ministry before marrying Amanda. Fearing she would call off the wedding, James had been afraid to tell his fiancée the truth. It was a stinging letdown. Amanda had married with the expectation of co-ministry, believing that James's work within the church would open up wider avenues of Christian service for them together.

A New Woman

I run in the path of your commands, for you have set my heart free. Psalm 119:32

*R*aise up your heart after a fall, sweetly and gently, humbling yourself before God in the knowledge of your misery," the charitable French bishop Francis de Sales counseled wisely, "and do not be astonished at your weakness, since it is not surprising that weakness should be weak, infirmity firm, and frailty frail."[6] In the trying years and hard economic times that followed, Amanda confessed that she struggled with constant challenges to her commitment to Christ. Passionately praying for the Lord's enduring grace, Amanda was determined to hold fast to her faith.

As James's desire to serve Christ withered, Amanda's bloomed. God's continued reaffirmations of His love provided a steady source of hope and comfort.

In September 1868, Amanda was led to worship at Green Street Church in Philadelphia. Seeking a spiritual confirmation from God known as sanctification, she vividly describes her remarkable reaction to Pastor John Inskip's teaching:

> Just then such a wave came over me, and such a welling up in my heart, and these words rang through me like a bell: *God in you, God in you*, and I thought, *doing what? Ruling every ambition and desire, and bringing every thought into captivity and obedience to His will.* How I have lived through it I cannot tell, but the blessedness of the love and the peace and power I can never describe. O, what glory filled my soul! The great vacuum in my soul began to fill up; it was like a pleasant draught of cool water, and I felt it. I wanted to shout Glory to Jesus![7]

Surrendering to God's sweet impartation of grace, Amanda notes "as quick as the spark from smitten steel I felt the touch of God from the crown of my head to the soles of my feet, and the welling up came." Leaving the service, she encountered the Holy Spirit once more:

> I don't know just how I looked, but I felt so wonderfully strange, yet I felt glorious. One of the good official brethren at the door said as I was passing out, "Well, auntie, how did you like that sermon?" but I could not speak; if I had, I should have shouted, but I simply nodded my head. Just as I put my foot on the top step I seemed to feel a hand, the touch of which I cannot describe. It seemed to

press me gently on the top of my head, and I felt something part and roll down and cover me like a great cloak! I felt it distinctly; it was done in a moment, and O what a mighty peace and power took possession of me![8]

Sharing the Wealth

> *I have hidden your word in my heart that I might not sin against you.* Psalm 119:11

manda's life-changing encounter with God convinced her that the Lord was finally in control of her life. No longer afraid of anyone, "not even white people," she was confident that her Savior had sanctified her soul, and she surrendered to the Holy Spirit's transforming power.

The godly disciple thirsted for fellowship with Jesus and found Him waiting to teach her as she went about her daily work. In the midst of her most menial tasks, Amanda prayed for insight and strength. In this way, she learned to face the Enemy of her soul without flinching, and was trained for future service in God's kingdom. To support her family, she sometimes stood by her washtub from six in the morning until six the next morning doing laundry, taking little naps as she leaned upon the window ledge.

Whether washing the dishes, sweeping the floors, making the bed, or determining exactly how much ironing could be done with ten cents, worth of coal, Amanda depended on God to supply her needs. When her old pair of shoes would no longer keep her feet dry, she prayed — and three days later, a stranger at church gave her five dollars. If her family did not have enough food to eat, or she was mistreated by her people, she took the "knee route," her term for her practice of constantly kneeling to pray whenever the need arose.

No matter what her life circumstances, Amanda Smith drew close to God through prayer, and as a result, acquired lasting spiritual muscle.

Amanda was eager to evangelize. Rarely leaving the house without a stack of tracts to pass along, she soon became completely at ease with sharing the Gospel with people she met. Countless men and women responded by committing their lives to Christ. Blessed with a beautiful singing voice and the gift of preaching, Amanda's frequent presence at revival meetings reached many hearts. Submitting herself to the will of the Almighty, God granted her the opportunity to serve Him every day.

Sowing Generously

I will walk about in freedom, for I have sought out your precepts. Psalm 119:45

She was an unusual sight in post-Civil War America — a black woman evangelist, an ex-slave, traversing North and South preaching to all races and then spending fourteen years . . . evangelizing in England, India and Africa," observes Elliott Wright in his book *Holy Company: Christian Heroes and Heroines.*[9] Yet until 1869, Amanda's ministry centered exclusively on churches near her home.

When her second husband passed away, she was ready to receive new orders. Upon hearing God's call to minister at meetings in New Jersey, Amanda quickly obeyed the Holy Spirit's leading, locked up her New York apartment, and headed out on an evangelistic journey that lasted seven months. By 1870, Amanda had started a full-time ministry. Though invitations to speak and sing at revival meetings across the country came in regularly, contributions to Amanda's ministry were sparse. Domestic "tent-making" work provided needed funds, and like the apostle Paul, Amanda embraced God's provision wholeheartedly.

When the African Methodist Episcopal Church held its first general conference south of the Mason-Dixon line, Amanda decided to attend even though women were not permitted to be delegates. Neither a feminist nor an agitator for women's ordination, she admitted, "The thought of ordination had never once entered my mind, for I had received my ordination from Him, Who said, 'Ye have not chosen me, but I have chosen you and ordained you, that you might go and bring forth good fruit.'"[10]

Before leaving for the Knoxville meeting, however, Amanda realized that racial hostilities might break into violence at any time. Kneeling, she prayed for guidance and protection: "Lord, if being a martyr for Thee would glorify Thee, all right; just to go down there and be butchered by wicked men for their own gratification, without any reference to Thy glory, I'm not willing. And now, Lord, help me. If Thou dost want me to do this, even then, give me the grace and enable me to do it."[11] Upon hearing the words, "My grace is sufficient for thee," she got up, satisfied with the Lord's reply and, without fear, departed for the historic assembly.

In the course of time, Amanda was called to foreign missions. On two separate occasions — at a church camp in Oakington, Maryland, in July 1870 and the Sea Cliff Camp Meeting in July 1872 — Amanda sensed that God was urging her to go to India and Africa, though many years passed before she was able to follow this conviction.

An invitation to preach in Great Britain came first.

Across the Atlantic

> *Your promises have been thoroughly tested,*
> *and your servant loves them.* Psalm 199:140

*I*n 1878, when the door opened for Amanda to minister in England, she faced a new identity crisis. "Go to England, Amanda Smith, the colored washwoman, go to England. No, I am not going to pray a bit," she argued with herself, "I have to ask the Lord for so many things I really need, that I'm not going to ask Him for what I don't need — to go to England. It does well enough for swell people to go, not for me."[12]

Convicted by the Holy Spirit for her lack of trust in God, Amanda understood why she did not want to go to England: She was afraid to cross the Atlantic Ocean. Then the Lord's goodness passed before her in a sweeping vision, and she knew that just as He had answered her prayers and provided for her every need in the past, He would continue to do so in a foreign land far away from her home. Filled with shame, she cried out, "Lord, forgive me, for Jesus' sake, and give me another chance, and I will go to England."

With her first-class passage paid for by friends who were excited about Amanda's deepening relationship with Christ, she sailed alone for Great Britain, claiming the promise found in Philippians (4:19 KJV): "My God shall supply all your need according to his riches in glory by Jesus Christ." Throughout the voyage, she enjoyed rewarding fellowship with God. To her delighted surprise, the ship's captain asked her to conduct the Sunday service, as there were no other ministers aboard the vessel. Testifying that "The Lord helped me to speak, sing, and pray," the willing preacher noted that people who had barely noticed her before crowded around her after the service. Though some initially considered her to be an unacceptable minister of the Gospel, Amanda was warmly regarded by everyone on board before the trip's end.

After her arrival at Liverpool, Amanda went to Keswick, where a large evangelical convention was taking place. There, she discovered, race did not matter. Accepted on the basis of her inspiring ministry, the determined evangelist spent twenty months preaching throughout England and then departed for Scotland, where she preached in Perth, Glasgow, Edinburgh, Aberdeen, and many more places. Originally planned as a three-month excursion, the trip ended up lasting two years.

The enthusiastic reception Amanda received in Great Britain was a welcome change. While her autobiography mentions the frequent racial hostility and sexual discrimination she faced while ministering to American Christians — including exclusion from meetings and severe housing restrictions — the missionary was treated kindly in Britain, where many people admired her uniqueness. Entertaining Amanda even became fashionable. Thus, God enabled His consecrated servant to share Jesus' Gospel within the uppermost circles of British society.

New Horizons

Direct my footsteps according to your word;
let no sin rule over me. Psalm 119:133

Convinced by an English friend's proposal to join a missions trip in 1879, Amanda reported that "the Lord marvelously opened the way for me to visit India." Her supporters' generous donations provided enough money to cover all the evangelist's expenses, including the cost of Mazie's room and board in America. The arduous days of washing and ironing to supply funds had ended.

When Amanda arrived in Bombay, the poverty she saw gripped her heart instantly. She was especially disturbed by the devastating conditions facing India's women, who were deprived of their human rights, and frequently experienced mistreatment by male relatives.

It was at an orphanage in the city of Colar that Amanda realized that evangelism in India must go hand in hand with meeting the people's physical needs, an understanding that influenced her work over the remaining years of her lifetime.

After a brief trip to England, Amanda embarked for Liberia. Arriving at the African colony where many former American slaves had been relocated, she helped to organize the Gospel Temperance Band, once again staying much longer than expected. During her eight years there, "many hearts were made whole," according to Amanda, where her ministry of music, preaching, and encouragement touched people from many denominations she had not worked with before. Her extended service exacted a high toll: Suffering repeated bouts of fever and illness, Amanda was eventually forced to retire from all her missionary work.

Stopping for the last time in England in 1890, the physically debilitated evangelist visited many of her old friends before permanently returning to the United States. But Amanda refused to succumb to any kind of idleness. Keeping up her previous intense pace, she continued preaching at church services and camp meetings throughout the East for two more years.

In 1892, at a friend's request, Amanda finally relocated to a temperance community near Chicago and proceeded to work on her memoirs, producing a collection of eyewitness accounts told in the authentic voice of a self-taught writer anointed by God. As the nineteenth century drew to a close, she was busy working with African-American orphans in Harvey, a suburb of Chicago, where she organized and opened the Amanda Smith Children's Home in

1899 with the first payment financed from the sales of her book and evangelistic ministry. Shortly after her retirement in 1912, Amanda went to Florida to live in a home provided by an affluent real estate investor, George Sebring, from where she departed to be with the Lord in February 1915.

"The penetrating power of discernment which she possessed in so large degree impressed me more and more the longer I knew her," a missionary in India, the Bishop James Thoburn, said of Amanda. "Indeed, through my association with her I learned many valuable lessons, more that has been of actual value to me as a preacher of Christian truth than from any other person I have ever met."[13] Wearing a Quaker wrapper made of brown or black cloth, with her head covered by a drab bonnet, she carried her meager belongings in a single carpetbag, speaking to people of all economic classes. How many of these lives did this plainspoken woman's service to God influence for Christ's kingdom?

Lord, speak to me, that I may speak
In living echoes of Thy tone;
As Thou hast sought, so let me seek
Thy erring children lost and lone.
O teach me, Lord, that I may teach
The precious things Thou dost impart;
And wing my words, that they may reach
The hidden depths of many a heart.
O fill me with Thy fullness, Lord,
Until my very heart o'erflow
In kindling thought and glowing word
Thy love to tell, Thy praise to show.
O use me, Lord, use even me,
Just as Thou wilt and where;
Until Thy blessed face I see,
Thy rest, Thy joy, Thy glory share.

— Frances Ridley Havergal (1836–1879)
"Lord, Speak to Me"

CONCLUSION

*Y*ou did not choose me: I chose you." Is not this what the grace of service is really all about? Whether we are young teens or senior citizens, salaried staff persons or voluntary workers, lifelong Christians or newly baptized believers, are we not like Ruth and Amanda, called to faithful ministry? Not because we feel like it; not even because we choose it; but because our Lord specifically gives us the task He has called us to do.

Throughout *Women of Character*, I have shared just a few of my favorite saints' stories — true tales of noble women who, against all odds, were given the grace to follow God's call: Mary of Magdala, who would not quit; Susanna, who would not submit; Rahab, who did not doubt; Ruth, who did not desert; Mary, who surrendered all; Pelagia, who kept nothing; Ramabai, who gained the treasure; Teresa, who sacrificed her life; Amanda, who found freedom; Abigail, who lost her home; Perpetua, who defeated the Devil; Mary of Bethany, who won her Lord. And they are not isolated witnesses. For countless generations, going all the way back to the beginning, women have played their part in filling the earth and subduing it with their love and labor. Their constant courage fills me with amazement and clears my sight.

But there is more: These saints' lives provoke my spiritual hunger. Their boldness makes me bolder. God chose each of these women to do something special. As I watch His plan for their lives unfolding, I see that it is true for me too.

The pattern is in place. I look back and I can see it.

Sometimes, when I ponder my position, I tremble. As you may have noticed, in all of these stories, the telltale signs of God's promotion (at least on this side of heaven) often appear in the form of persecutions, suffering, hardships, loneliness, and catastrophes, from which a death-defying experience of peace and joy inexplicably rises. I do not doubt this reality. Over and again, saints show us, by the tenacious veracity of their lives, that sharing in Christ's sufferings delivers a crown of honor. Our heavenly Father reigns triumphant over His creation no matter how bleak the landscape grows.

The Bible teaches me this, I know. Still, when I read about other Christians' lives from start to finish and add their accounts to what the Scriptures tell me about following Jesus, I gain greater confidence to face my own life's seasons. I discover that brokenness, not positive thinking, is the best preparation for lasting growth. There is no permanent substitute for patience and perseverance along the pilgrim way.

"If I want potatoes for dinner tomorrow, it will do me little good to plant them in my garden tonight," confirms Dr. Eugene Peterson in *Earth and Altar*. "There are long stretches of darkness and invisibility that separate planting and reaping. During the stretches of waiting, there is cultivating and weeding and nurturing and planting still other seeds."[14]

Notice how this principle conspicuously applies to the best and brightest of our profession, the great women of our faith. See their loneliness deeply dig down into their heart's hardness, furrowing out the Spirit's planting place; watch as a minuscule seed dissolves, sprouts, takes root, and punches through thick earthy layers, reaching for heaven; wait for the final scene, when the tiny shoot, now transformed into a towering stalk, is reaped by the Harvester's scythe as He gathers His fully ripened crop. "Unless a kernel of wheat falls to the ground and dies ..." (John 12:24).

The Hebrews' epistle is right: As I stretch toward the finish line, it helps to know that the bleachers on my side are brimming with unseen heroes to whom the race matters.

The root system needed to support a mature maple tree must spread out far below the topsoil to promote survival; what is seen above the ground rises up in proportion to what lies beneath the standing timber. This, I think, is also true of the women saints who inspire us the most: Their hidden life of prayer and devotion shaped what was outwardly visible. A formidable, inner strength, produced by the Holy Spirit and reinforced by their desire for intimacy with Christ, nourished their active ministry, which stood above the rest on the surface. Unseen aspects of their lives — private prayer, solitary worship, secret gifts, silent tears — exceeded their public displays of piety. Our feminine predecessors' intact root systems teach today's saints valuable lessons.

"It does not take great men to do great things; it only takes consecrated men,"[15] the famous nineteenth-century pastor and hymn writer Phillips Brooks discovered. The timeless norm of women's ministry, that uncommon kind of faithful abiding we see in such surprisingly diverse places as a crowded Roman prison or Bethlehem's harvest fields, is characterized by the distinctly Christian qualities of gentleness, humility, kindness, patience, and compassion. Jesus leads; we follow.

Like the women saints who came before us, our value to the Lord is not measured by the size of our paycheck, the sum of our earnings, the status of our position. Kneeling before Christ's throne — with nothing to offer but ourselves — by God's grace, we are sent forth in His service.

I wonder: Where will He lead us?

Points for Reflection

1. Realizing that God wants me, not my success, means . . .
2. Serving the Lord without resentment is only possible when . . .
3. Ruth's relationship with Naomi reminds me of . . .
4. My upbringing taught me to expect to grow up to be . . .
5. Amanda's story seemed particularly joyful at the point where . . .
6. Faith is related to serving Christ in the sense that . . .

Prayer: Heavenly Father, I ask for Your help and guidance today. Give me grace to serve You wholeheartedly; show me how to use my time wisely. Knowing that You are here with me — my strength, my life, my comfort — sustains my heart. I praise You and thank You for the blessing of Your presence, now and always, through Jesus Christ. Amen.

The law of the LORD is perfect,
reviving the soul.
The statutes of the LORD are trustworthy,
making wise the simple.
The precepts of the LORD are right,
giving joy to the heart.
The commands of the LORD are radiant,
giving light to the eyes.
The fear of the LORD is pure,
enduring forever.
The ordinances of the LORD are sure
and altogether righteous.
They are more precious than gold,
than much pure gold;
they are sweeter than honey,
than honey from the comb.
By them is your servant warned;
in keeping them there is great reward.

— Psalm 19:7–11

I am glad to think
I am not bound to make the world go right,
but only to discover and to do
With cheerful heart the work that God appoints.
I will trust him
That he can hold his own; and I will take
His will, above the work he sendeth me,
To be my chiefest good.

— Jean Ingelow (1820–1897)

Paradise: In A Dream

(Lyra Messianica, second edition, 1865)

*Once in a dream I saw the flowers
That bud and bloom in Paradise;
More fair they are than waking eyes
Have seen in all this world of ours.
And faint the perfume-bearing rose,
And faint the lily on its stem,
And faint the perfect violet
Compared with them.
I heard the songs of Paradise:
Each bird sat singing in its place;
A tender song so full of grace
It soared like incense to the skies.
Each bird sat singing to his mate
Soft cooing notes among the trees:
The nightingale herself were cold
To such as these.*

*I saw the fourfold River flow,
And deep it was, with golden sand;
It flowed between a mossy land
Which murmured music grave and low.
It hath refreshment for all thirst,
For fainting spirits strength and rest:
Earth holds not such a draught as this
From east to west.*

The Tree of life stood budding there,
Abundant with it twelvefold fruits ;
Eternal sap sustains its roots,
Its shadowing branches fill the air.
Its leaves are healing for the world,
Its fruit the hungry world can feed,
Sweeter than honey to the taste
And balm indeed.

I saw the gate called Beautiful;
And looked, but scarce could look, within;
I saw the golden streets begin,
And outskirts of the glassy pool.
Oh harps, oh crowns of plenteous stars,
Oh green palm-branches many-leaved —
Eye hath not seen, nor ear hath heard,
Nor heart conceived.

I hope to see these things again,
But not as once in dreams by night;
To see them with my very sight,
And touch and handle, and attain:
To have all heaven beneath my feet
For narrow way that once they trod;
To have my part with all the Saints,
And with my God.

—Christina Rossetti (1830–1894)

Notes

Introduction

1. St. John Chrysostom, quoted in *12,000 Religious Quotations*, Frank S. Mead, ed. (Grand Rapids: Baker, 1989), 299.

2. John White, *The Fight* (Downers Grove, Ill.: InterVarsity Press, 1976), 110.

3. To preserve each woman's confidentiality, I disguised their identities in one (or more) ways: by using pseudonyms, altering small details, and, in a few cases, combining two women's histories to form a representative composite. Despite these necessary alterations, I believe the essential elements of their stories remain unchanged.

Chapter One: *Brokenness*

1. M. Basilea Schlink, *Repentance — the Joy-filled Life*, trans. Harriet Corbin (Grand Rapids: Zondervan, 1968), 52.

2. Jean-Pierre de Caussade, *Spiritual Letters of Jean-Pierre de Caussade*, trans. Kitty Muggeridge (Wilton, Conn.: Morehouse-Barlow, 1986), 113.

3. Edith Schaeffer, *A Way of Seeing* (Old Tappan, N.J.: Revell, 1977), 144.

4. Paul Hiebert, "Pandita Ramabai: Mission to Hindu Women," in *Ambassadors for Christ*, John D. Woodbridge, ed. (Chicago: Moody Press, 1994), 168.

5. Edith Deen, *Great Women of the Christian Faith* (Uhrichsville, Ohio: Barbour and Company, Inc., 1959), 261.

6. Ruth A. Tucker and Walter Liefeld, *Daughters of the Church* (Grand Rapids: Academie/Zondervan, 1987), 344.

7. Ibid.

8. Hiebert, "Pandita Ramabai: Mission to Hindu Women," 169.

9. Pandita Ramabai, *A Testimony*, 9th ed. (Kedgaon, Poona Dist., India: Ramabai Mukti Mission, 1968), quoted in *In Her Words: Women's Writings in the History of Christian Thought*, Amy Oden, ed. (Nashville, Tenn.: Abingdon, 1994), 326.

10. Hiebert, "Pandita Ramabai: Mission to Hindu Women," 170.

11. Ramabai, *A Testimony*, quoted in Oden, *In Her Words*, 327.

12. Hiebert, 173.

13. J. I. Packer, *Knowing God*, rev. ed. (Downers Grove, Ill.: Inter-Varsity Press, 1993), 250.

14. Jean-Pierre de Caussade, quoted in *The Joy of the Saints*, ed. Robert L. Llewelyn (Springfield, Ill.: Templegate, 1988), 353.

Chapter Two: *Belief*

1. Jeremy Taylor, quoted in Mead, *12,000 Religious Quotations*, 137.

2. *The Lives of the Spiritual Mothers* (Buena Vista, Colo.: Holy Apostles Convent, 1991), 458.

3. Ibid., 458–59.

4. Ibid., 460.

5. Ibid., 461.

6. Ibid., 461.

7. Angela Merici, quoted in *The Wisdom of the Saints*, Jill Haak Adels, ed. (Oxford: Oxford University Press, 1987), 145.

8. *The Lives of the Spiritual Mothers*, 463.

9. Ibid., 465.

10. Dick Keyes, *Beyond Identity: Finding Your Self in the Image and Character of God* (Ann Arbor, Mich.: Servant, 1984), 97.

11. Ibid., 99.

12. John Newton, quoted in *In Search of God*, David C. K. Watson (London: Falcon Books, 1974), 101.

Chapter Three: *Surrender*

1. Philip Neri, quoted in Adels, *The Wisdom of the Saints*, 32.

2. Jill Briscoe, *Songs from Heaven and Earth* (Nashville, Tenn.: Nelson, 1985), 25.

3. Charles de Foucald, quoted in *The Oxford Book of Prayers*, George Appleton, ed. (New York: Oxford University Press, 1985), 85.

4. Deen, *Great Women of the Christian Faith*, 4.

5. Vibia Perpetua, *The Martyrdom of Perpetua*, quoted in *In Her Words*, 28.

6. Edward Hubbell Chapin, quoted in Mead, *12,000 Religious Quotations*, 412.

7. Perpetua, *The Martyrdom of Perpetua*, quoted in Oden, *In Her Words*, 29.

8. Deen, *Great Women of the Christian Faith*, 5.

9. Ibid., 4.

10. Ibid., 5.

11. Ibid., 6.

12. Patricia Wilson-Kastner, *A Lost Tradition: Women Writers of the Early Church* (Lanham, New York and London: University Press of America, 1981), 4.

13. David Hugh Farmer, *The Oxford Dictionary of Saints*, 3rd. ed. (Oxford: Oxford University Press, 1992), 386.

14. Wilson-Kastner, *A Lost Tradition: Women Writers of the Early Church.*

15. W. Ian Thomas, *The Saving Life of Christ* (Grand Rapids: Zondervan, 1961), 18.

16. Ibid.

17. Philip Henry, quoted in Mead, *12,000 Religious Quotations*, 22.

Chapter Four: *Obedience*

1. William Wilberforce, *Real Christianity* (Portland, Ore.: Multnomah Press, 1982), 47.

2. Matthew Henry, quoted in Mead, *12,000 Religious Quotations*, 2.

3. Phillips Brooks, quoted in Mead, *12,000 Religious Quotations*, 320.

4. Eugene H. Peterson, *Praying with Jesus* (San Francisco: Harper San Francisco, 1993), November 9.

5. E. Paul Hovey, quoted in Mead, *12,000 Religious Quotations*, 228.

Chapter Five: *Devotion*

1. St. Augustine, quoted in Mead, *12,000 Religious Quotations*, 275.

2. Anne Morrow Lindbergh, *Gift from the Sea* (New York: Random House, 1975), 55–56.

3. Charles Colson, *Loving God* (Grand Rapids: Zondervan, 1983), 25.

4. Phillips Brooks, quoted in Mead, *12,000 Religious Quotations*, 50.

5. Teresa of Avila, *The Life of Teresa of Jesus: The Autobiography of Teresa of Avila* (New York: Image/Doubleday, 1991), 69.

6. Ibid., 66.

7. Ibid., 65.

8. Ibid., 74.

9. Ibid., 77–78.

10. Ibid., 95.

11. Ibid., 109.

12. Ibid., 118.

13. Tryon Edwards, quoted in Mead, *12,000 Religious Quotations*, 238.

14. Teresa of Avila, *The Life of Teresa of Jesus*, 357.

15. Teresa of Avila, quoted in Llewelyn, *The Joy of the Saints*, 289.

16. Caroline Marshall, "Teresa of Avila," in *Eerdmans' Handbook to the History of Christianity*, Tim Dowley, ed. (Grand Rapids: Eerdmans, 1977), 417.

17. E. Allison Peers, *Mother of Carmel* (Wilton, Conn.: Morehouse-Barlow, 1944), 6.

18. Clayton L. Berg, Jr., "Introduction," in St. Teresa's *A Life of Prayer*, James L. Houston, ed. (Portland, Ore.: Multnomah Press, 1983), xxxiii–xxxiv.

19. Teresa of Avila, quoted in Llewelyn, *The Joy of the Saints*, 186.

20. Houston, *A Life of Prayer*, xi.

21. C. S. Lewis, *Mere Christianity* (New York: Macmillan, 1960), 190.

22. Hannah More, quoted in Mead, *12,000 Religious Quotations*, 20.

Chapter Six: *Service*

1. Frederick William Robertson, quoted in Mead, *12,000 Religious Quotations*, 405.

2. Jonathan Edwards, quoted in Mead, *12,000 Religious Quotations*, 227.

3. Deen, *Great Women of the Christian Faith*, 32.

4. Tucker and Liefeld, *Daughters of the Church*, 270.

5. Deen, *Great Women of the Christian Faith*, 233.

6. Francis de Sales, quoted in Llewelyn, *The Joy of the Saints*, 351.

7. Amanda Smith, *An Autobiography: The Story of the Lord's Dealings with Amanda Smith* (London: Hodder and Stoughton, 1894), quoted in Oden, *In Her Words*, 310.

8. Ibid., 311.

9. Elliott Wright, *Holy Company: Christian Heroes and Heroines* (New York: Macmillan, 1980), 39–40.

10. Tucker and Liefeld, *Daughters of the Church*, 271.

11. Deen, *Great Women of the Christian Faith*, 237.

12. Ibid.

13. Wright, *Holy Company*, 42.

14. Eugene H. Peterson, *Earth and Altar* (Downers Grove, Ill.: InterVarsity Press, 1985).

15. Phillips Brooks, quoted in Mead, *12,000 Religious Quotations*, 86.

Bibliography

Adels, Jill Haak, ed. *The Wisdom of the Saints*. Oxford: Oxford University Press, 1987.

Bridges, Jerry. *The Pursuit of Holiness*. Colorado Springs: Nav-Press, 1978.

Briscoe, Jill. *Songs from Heaven and Earth*. Nashville: Nelson, 1985.

Chambers, Oswald. *My Utmost for His Highest*. New York: Dodd, Mead & Co., 1963.

Clark, Elizabeth. *Women in the Early Church. Message of the Fathers of the Church, no. 13*. Wilmington, Del.: Glazier, 1983.

Colson, Charles. *Loving God*. Grand Rapids: Zondervan, 1983.

de Caussade, Jean-Pierre. *Spiritual Letters of Jean-Pierre de Caussade*. Trans. Kitty Muggeridge. Wilton, Conn.: Morehouse-Barlow, 1986.

Deen, Edith. *All of the Women of the Bible*. San Francisco: HarperSanFrancisco, 1955.

_____. *Great Women of the Christian Faith*. Uhrichsville, Ohio: Barbour and Company, Inc., 1959.

Dowley, Tim, ed. *Eerdmans' Handbook to the History of Christianity*. Grand Rapids: Eerdmans, 1977.

Farmer, David Hugh. *The Oxford Dictionary of Saints, 3rd ed*. Oxford: Oxford University Press, 1992.

Foster, Richard J. *Prayer: Finding the Heart's True Home*. San Francisco: HarperSanFrancisco, 1992.

_____. *Prayers from the Heart*. San Francisco: HarperSanFrancisco, 1994.

Hiebert, Paul. "Pandita Ramabai: Mission to Hindu Women." In *Ambassadors for Christ*. Ed. John D. Woodbridge. Chicago: Moody Press, 1994.

Hill, Carolyn Miles, ed. *The World's Great Religious Poetry*. New York: Macmillan, 1941.

Keyes, Dick. *Beyond Identity: Finding Your Self in the Image and Character of God*. Ann Arbor, Mich.: Servant, 1984.

Lewis, C. S. *Mere Christianity*. New York: Macmillan, 1960.

Lindbergh, Anne Morrow. *Gift from the Sea*. New York: Random House, 1975.

Llewelyn, Robert L., ed. *The Joy of the Saints*. Springfield, Ill.: Templegate Publishers, 1988.

Macartney, Clarence Edward. *Great Women of the Bible*. Grand Rapids: Kregel, 1991.

Matheson, George. *Portraits of Bible Women*. Grand Rapids: Kregel, 1987.

Matthews, Victor H. *Manners and Customs in Bible Times*. Peabody, Mass.: Hendrickson Publishers, Inc., 1988.

Mead, Frank S., ed. *12,000 Religious Quotations*. Grand Rapids: Baker, 1989.

Miller, Calvin. *Walking with Saints*. Nashville: Nelson, 1995.

Morgan, Tom. *Saints*. San Francisco: Chronicle Books, 1994.

Oden, Amy, ed. *In Her Words: Women's Writings in the History of Christian Thought*. Nashville: Abingdon, 1994.

Packer, J. I. *Knowing God*, rev. ed. Downers Grove, Ill.: InterVarsity Press, 1993.

Peers, E. Allison. *Mother of Carmel*. Wilton, Conn.: Morehouse-Barlow, 1944.

Peterson, Eugene. *A Long Obedience in the Same Direction*. Downers Grove, Ill.: InterVarsity Press, 1980.

————. *Earth and Altar*. Downers Grove, Ill.: InterVarsity Press, 1985.

————. *Praying with Jesus*. San Francisco: HarperSanFrancisco, 1993, Nov. 9.

Ramabai, Pandita. *A Testimony*, 9th ed. Kedgoan, Poona Dist., India: Ramabai Mukti Mission, 1968.

Schaeffer, Edith. *A Way of Seeing*. Old Tappan, N.J.: Revell, 1977.

Schlink, M. Basilea. *Repentance — the Joy-filled Life*. Trans. Harriet Corbin. Grand Rapids: Zondervan, 1968.

Shelley, Bruce. *All the Saints Adore Thee*. Grand Rapids: Baker, 1988.

Smith, Amanda. *An Autobiography: The Story of the Lord's Dealings with Amanda Smith*. London: Hodder and Stoughton, 1894.

Sproul, R. C. *The Soul's Quest for God*. Wheaton, Ill.: Tyndale House, 1992.

Teresa of Avila. *The Collected Works of St. Teresa of Avila*. Trans. Kieran Kavanaugh and Otilio Rodriguez. Washington, D.C.: ICS Publications, 1976.

_____. *A Life of Prayer*. Ed. James L. Houston. Portland, Ore.: Multnomah Press, 1983.

_____. *The Life of Teresa of Jesus: The Autobiography of Teresa of Avila*. New York: Image/Doubleday, 1991.

Thomas, W. Ian. *The Saving Life of Christ*. Grand Rapids: Zondervan, 1961.

Toon, Peter. *Spiritual Companions: An Introduction to the Christian Classics*. Grand Rapids: Baker, 1990.

Tucker, Ruth A., and Walter Liefeld. *Daughters of the Church*. Grand Rapids: Academie/Zondervan, 1987.

Walsh, Michael, ed. *Butler's Lives of the Saints*. San Francisco: HarperSanFrancisco, 1991.

Watson, David C. K. *In Search of God*. London: Falcon Books, 1974.

Wesley, John. *The Gift of Love*. Ed. Arthur Skevington. London: Darton, Longman and Todd, 1988.

White, John. *The Fight*. Downers Grove, Ill.: InterVarsity Press, 1976.

White, Kristin E. *A Guide to the Saints*. New York: Ballantine Books, 1991.

Wilberforce, William. *Real Christianity*. Portland, Ore.: Multnomah Press, 1982.

Wilson-Kastner, Patricia. *A Lost Tradition: Women Writers of the Early Church*. Lanham, New York and London: University Press of America, 1981.

Woodridge, John D., ed. *Ambassadors for Christ: Distinguished Representatives of the Message Throughout the World*. Chicago: Moody Press, 1994.

Wright, Elliott. *Holy Company: Christian Heroes and Heroines*. New York: Macmillan, 1980.